Tips & Traps for Remodeling Your Kitchen

R. Dodge Woodson

McGRAW-HILL

New York   Chicago   San Francisco   Lisbon   London
Madrid   Mexico City   Milan   New Delhi   San Juan
Seoul   Singapore   Sydney   Toronto

The McGraw·Hill Companies

Cataloging-in-Publication Data is on file with the Library of Congress

1 2 3 4 5 6 7 8 9 0   DOC/DOC   0 1 0 9 8 7 6 5

ISBN 0-07-144586-2

The sponsoring editor for this book was Cary Sullivan and the production supervisor was Pamela A. Pelton. It was set in Garamond by Lone Wolf Enterprises, Ltd. The art director for the cover was Handel Low.

Printed and bound by RR Donnelley.

Interior clipart images courtesy of www.clipart.com.

McGraw-Hill books are available at special quantity discounts to use as premiums and sales promotions, or for use in corporate training programs. For more information, please write to the Director of Special Sales, McGraw-Hill Professional, Two Penn Plaza, New York, NY 10121-2298. Or contact your local bookstore.

 This book is printed on recycled, acid-free paper containing a minimum of 50% recycled, de-inked fiber.

Dedication

I dedicate this book to Adam and Afton, the two best children a father could ask for. Afton has supported my writing since my first book, and Adam has never complained about my need to finish a chapter before venturing into our woods. They truly are the best children I could have dreamed of.

Contents

CHAPTER 15

CHAPTER 16

About the Author

R. Dodge Woodson has been involved in the building trades for 30 years and has been a self-employed contractor for 25 years. He is the owner of The Masters Group, Inc., a general contracting, remodeling, and plumbing firm in Maine. Woodson has written dozens of books on the industry for both consumers and professionals.

Introduction

A re you thinking of hiring a general contractor for home improvements or remodeling? Has the thought of saving thousands of dollars by being your own general contractor crossed your mind? Most homeowners seeking to improve their homes either hire a general contractor or act as their own construction manager while hiring subcontractors. In either case, this book is one of the most important tools that will be found on the job site.

Adding space to your home or improving existing living conditions can be a very traumatic time. But, it doesn't have to be. With the right knowledge, you can maintain control of your job. It will be easier on you to hire a general contractor, but there is a lot of money to be saved if you act as your own general contractor.

Almost anyone researching the rules of the road for remodeling has discovered horror stories about doing business with contractors and subcontractors. These stories are true. R. Dodge Woodson, the author, has been in the business for 30 years. He shares many of his own experiences on these pages. Best of all, he tells readers what to watch out for and how to avoid costly mistakes before, during, and after a home improvement or remodeling job.

Woodson has compiled a career of information here to help and protect you. For the mere cost of this book, you may save thousands of dollars on your job. Even more important, it is likely that you will avert disaster by not making the types of mistakes that many homeowners and inexperienced general contractors make.

Thumb through these pages. Notice the bullet lists, the tip boxes, and the numerous sample forms. The author has taken a serious, complicated subject and turned it into an accessible, easy-to-understand guide for homeowners. The writing is concise and the illustrations point out key factors toward a successful job.

You don't have to be a victim of unscrupulous contractors. Woodson will show you how to avoid them. Additionally, you will learn how to manage reputable contractors and assure yourself of quality work that comes in on budget and on time. Your home may be your single largest investment; don't risk it to renegade contractors. Learn how to protect yourself, your finances, and your home with this reader-friendly roadmap to success.

Go ahead and spend a little time looking over the chapters. It will not take long to see the value of Woodson's invaluable experience and advice. You don't have to go it alone. Take the words of a veteran contractor with you along every step of your remodeling adventure. Pick and choose the topics that you need, but don't go home without this essential element of your new project.

1

Planning Your Job

The planning phase of your kitchen remodeling project is very important. In fact, proper planning is the key to success in any remodeling venture. It is during this phase that the mold is cast for your entire job. If a mistake is made in the planning phase, the result can be both dissatisfying and costly.

Why is planning so important? Planning is critical to a successful remodeling job for several reasons. It allows you to establish a budget, a timetable, and a goal for the desired results. For example, if you are working on a limited budget as most homeowners are, it will be necessary to separate your needs from your desires.

Defining an accurate timetable can be crucial in kitchen remodeling. Since few homes have more than one kitchen, a major remodel can mean many trips to restaurants, and that gets expensive. Under these circumstances the timetable for remodeling your kitchen not only affects your convenience. It also affects your overall job cost, since those trips to restaurants will add up.

A PLAN

Before you begin to tear out kitchen cabinets, it helps to have a plan for their replacement. If you go into a major remodeling job without a plan for the finished product, you are not likely to enjoy the experience. Can you imagine ripping out your kitchen cabinets only to find out that the replacements that you thought could be picked up at the store will really take six weeks to get? Could you live with a dysfunctional kitchen for six weeks? You could, but it wouldn't be fun.

Planning a major remodeling job is not something you do on a Saturday afternoon. Proper planning takes time and effort. There will be phone calls to make, specifications to draft, and much more. What else will you need to do in the planning phase? This chapter is going to show you step by step what to do and how to do it. Once you have finished this chapter, you will be much better prepared to plan your job.

Kitchens are one of the best rooms in a home to remodel when you are thinking of recovering the cost of your investment.

NEEDS AND DESIRES

Remodeling jobs evolve from either needs or desires, and you should identify the difference between them before you make financial commitments. If you are planning to remodel your kitchen, you are fortunate in your choice of rooms. The kitchen is normally considered the most important room in a home to remodel.

If you review statistics on which types of remodeling jobs are most likely to pay for themselves when a home is sold, you will see that kitchens and bathrooms normally control the first two spots on the charts. This knowledge is comforting, but don't allow it to lull you into a false sense of security. While it is true that bathrooms and kitchens are great places to invest your improvement money, you must invest wisely.

Figure 1.1 Elaborately designed kitchens require especially careful planning. *Courtesy of Wellborn Cabinet, Inc.*

Kitchens are expected to have certain components. They should be equipped with cabinets, counters, sinks, and appliances. These are the most basic essentials, and there are many more suitable elements that could be included in kitchens. There are a host of add-on products available that are not mandatory equipment. To cull the crop of possibilities, you must separate your needs from your desires. To understand the difference between a need and a desire, let's look at an example for a typical kitchen-remodeling job.

Investing too much in any project can result in lost money, and so can installing non-conforming products and materials.

Assume that you have a standard kitchen that you want to update. We will call it a basic galley-style kitchen. You have the basics, but none of the frills. There is an old stainless-steel sink, 20-year-old ugly cabinets, a cracked counter, and nothing that makes you happy. The existing floor structure is in good condition, but the old vinyl flooring is worn and dull. The walls and ceiling are painted drywall, and there is an old range vent that sticks out of the wall with grease-stained rusted metal around it. The room is functional but unpleasing to the eye. What will you do to give this room a facelift?

If you want to make a safe investment, you will not get carried away with fancy options. You will make improvements, but they will be simple and relatively inexpensive. For example, you will replace the sink with a new one, but you will not use a cast-iron sink or a granite counter. While both of these options are beautiful and pleasant to use, the return on your investment could suffer. Of course, this depends on the nature of your home and its location.

The decision of how far to take your improvements has to be based on local conditions. You don't want to be the only home on the street that does not have a certain type of kitchen. Once you make the decision to improve your kitchen, do it right. A mistake would be to invest in custom cabinets, granite tops, a cast-iron sink, big-ticket faucets, and tile when competitive homes have stainless-steel sinks, modest faucets, and composite counters.

You will want to repaint the walls and ceiling and replace the old floor covering with new vinyl flooring. If you have fluorescent lights, get rid of them. Use something like recessed lighting, under-the-cabinet lights, and track lighting to dress up the room.

If you follow the above procedures, you could hardly go wrong. The kitchen will be modernized and functional without being luxurious or expensive. This type of remodeling will meet all common needs, and it will likely return most of its cost when you sell your house. But is this what you want to do?

Figure 1.2   Simple, functional design is apparent in this attractive kitchen. *Courtesy of Armstrong*

Suppose you want to replace the cabinets with etched-glass doors on your new cabinets, corner cabinets to extend your work area, island cabinets, and a host of other visual enhancements. How would that affect your job? This could be good, but will it? You have to investigate your decisions. With the example I have given you, it sounds like a viable plan. Counter space is always a welcome addition to a kitchen.

This type of needs-vs.-desires evaluation will enable you to realize your goals without busting your budget. It is easy to become enthralled with the excitement of getting a new kitchen, but you must temper the excitement with logic and sound judgment. While many upgrades, such as wallpaper and tile, may be fine for your project, don't allow your dreams to exceed your financial capabilities and expectations.

BUILDING A VIABLE BUDGET

Building a viable budget for a remodeling project is not always easy. Every time you visit a store or thumb through a remodeling magazine, your wish list can grow. Unless money is no object in your project, self-discipline must prevail over sudden emotions. Building a budget will take time and effort, but it will also protect you from financial disasters.

Don't begin any work until you have a viable budget and cost projections that fall within that budget. Starting a job without this information is likely to result in a very expensive lesson that you would prefer not to learn from firsthand experience.

How Will a Budget Protect You?

How will a budget protect you? A budget, broken down by categories, will define your parameters for each type of expense involved with your job. For example, if you have budgeted $150 for a stainless-steel kitchen sink, you will not, or at least you should not, spend $500 for a cast-iron sink in a high-fashion color. Setting up your budget in phases will help keep your spending patterns on track.

How Will You Develop Your Budget?

How will you develop your budget? A good budget will start at the beginning and include every phase of work to be done. It will be broken down into several categories, and it will be laid out to show projected costs and actual costs.

The more detailed the budget breakdowns are, the better off you will be. For example, you could have a broad category, such as plumbing, or you could break it down into smaller sections. In the case of plumbing, you might have a subcategory for labor, fixtures, and rough materials. This would be helpful if you are doing your own plumbing, but if you are hiring a contractor, the budget breakdown might be different.

It is wise to include a budget amount for each plumbing fixture. Looking at lump-sum figures is not always as graphic as seeing the item-by-item costs. If you see quotes from three plumbers for $3,500, you might mumble about the high cost but not know if the price could be reduced. When you can see that you are paying $125 for a sink, $155 for a faucet, and $400 for the labor to hook up your dishwasher, you can begin to evaluate the options you have. Seeing individual prices will allow you to alter your plans to maintain your budget.

If you don't establish a viable budget, your job's cost could get out of hand and result in an unpleasant experience. Before you run all over town writing checks and charging materials, you should know, within a reasonable variance, what the total of your expenditures will be.

When hiring a contractor, you should work with quoted prices for the services and materials to be provided. Under these circumstances, the breakdown between labor and rough materials is not very important. You are able to work with firm quotes and contracts that should detail all specifications for the work being done.

FINANCING THE WORK

Kitchen remodeling can get very expensive, and for most people this necessitates financing the work. While some people detest the idea of financing anything, some types of home-improvement financing may work to your advantage.

Equity Loans

Getting an equity loan on your home to pay for the work could result in some tax advantages for you. Not only is it possible that the interest paid on this type of loan is tax-deductible, but it is also a sure bet that you will still have your cash. If you can structure financing that offers tax advantages and invest your cash wisely in other areas, you may come out ahead of the game.

In-Home Financing

Many contractors have relationships with lenders that allow you to take advantage of in-home financing. The rates and terms of

Figure 1.3 Beautiful amenities must be included in a viable budget. *Courtesy of Armstrong*

this type of financing are usually not as good as what you could obtain from your own bank, but there are times when this type of loan may be justified. If you decide to accept in-home financing, make sure that you understand all the terms and conditions. You should have an attorney review the paperwork and render an opinion on it before signing on the dotted line.

PLANS AND SPECIFICATIONS

While simple remodeling will not require the use of complex blueprints, it is necessary to have a set of plans, even if they are only simple line drawings and specifications for the work you want done, especially if contractors will be doing the work for you.

It is impossible to obtain accurate bids from contractors unless they are provided with identical plans and specifications. If you don't provide detailed plans and specifications, the contractors may all bid the job based on different interpretations. The result will be bids that cannot be compared fairly.

Some people don't have the artistic ability to draw working plans, but all homeowners can create detailed specifications for their jobs. You can have professionals draw your plans for you, but you must create your own specifications. Nobody else knows what you want. This part of your planning is essential, and it should be done before bids for labor and materials are sought.

> Require all contractors bidding your work to provide a detailed outline of the work and products that they will be providing you for a set price. Make sure that all contractors have identical plans and specifications to work with when working up your quotes.

PLANNING FOR INCONVENIENCES

Planning for inconveniences is a part of any remodeling job, but it is especially applicable to kitchens and bathrooms. If you were having your basement converted to finished living space, you would have to put up with noise, dust, and the traffic of contractors, but the level of inconvenience with kitchen remodeling exceeds that of most other forms of remodeling.

To avoid going hungry, you should plan for known inconveniences. If your plans call for a total kitchen renovation, it is logical to assume that you may be without cooking facilities for a few days. The time could be much longer, depending upon your contractor.

In the case of major kitchen renovations, cooking may be out of the question for several days, possibly weeks. When your old kitchen cabinets are removed, where will you put all the items that were stored in them? Having contractors stand around, mumbling and tapping their feet, while you box up food, utensils, and small appliances can add to the stress big

Kitchen Remodeling Notes

Customer s Name: _____

Customer s Address: _____

Job Address: _____

Customer s Phone Number: _____

What type of space is below the kitchen? Is it a basement or other living space?

_____

What type of space is above the kitchen? It is attic space or living space?

_____

Are there kitchen doors? _____

What types of doors are installed _____

What types of windows are existing? _____

What type of flooring exists in the kitchen? _____

Does the subfloor seem solid? _____

What are the dimensions of the floor? _____

What are the dimensions of the ceiling? _____

What are the dimensions of the wall areas? _____

What is the cabinet layout? _____

What type of sink is existing? _____

What type of countertop is existing? _____

Is there an existing dishwasher? _____

Figure 1.4   Kitchen remodeling notes

Is there an existing garbage disposer? _____

Is there an existing icemaker in the freezer of the refrigerator? _____

Does the water pipe for the sink come out of the wall or out of the floor? _____

What type of drain pipes are existing? _____

Does the drain come through the floor or the wall? _____

What type of sink is wanted? _____

What type of faucets are wanted? _____

What type of water pipe is existing? _____

Is there any exposed plumbing along the walls or baseboards? _____

Will plumbing fixtures be going back into the same locations, or will they be moved?

What type of roof does the house have? _____

Is there a GFI circuit for the kitchen? _____

How far apart are the outlets around the countertop? _____

What type of light fixtures are existing? _____

What type of heat is in the kitchen? _____

How far is the electrical panel from the bathroom? _____

What is the access for running wires to the panel? _____

What brand of circuit breakers are being used? _____

Is the electrical panel 100-amp or 200-amp? _____

Does the electrical box appear to have blank spaces available in it? _____

Does any of the heat need to be moved? _____

What type of walls are existing? _____

Figure 1.4 (*continued*)   Kitchen remodeling notes

What type of ceiling is existing? _____

Do the walls and floor seem level and plumb? _____

How difficult will the ripout be to get out of the house? _____

How is the access for hauling away debris? _____

What type of flooring is wanted? _____

What brand and type of plumbing fixtures are wanted? _____

What types of cabinets are wanted? _____

What is the kitchen layout? _____

Are new appliances wanted? _____

What types of walls will be used? _____

What type of ceiling will be used? _____

Is ceramic tile needed? _____

What type of countertop is wanted? _____

Are there any skylights to work around? _____

What type of accessories are needed?

What type of wall covering, such as paint, is wanted? _____

What type of trim will be installed? _____

What do we need to trim? _____

Are we painting or staining the trim? _____

NOTES:

_____

Figure 1.4 (*continued*)   Kitchen remodeling notes

remodeling jobs are known to come with. Proper planning allows you to avoid this type of stressful, and sometimes embarrassing, situation.

Before you begin your remodeling project, sit down and draw a mental picture of how the job will go. If you don't know enough about what will be done to create a plausible picture, ask your contractors to explain the sequence of events. If necessary, outline the work on a piece of paper. This may help you to see and avoid complications before they happen. For example, assume the electrical wiring in your kitchen is going to be updated. What will happen to the food in your refrigerator and freezer? Can you use an extension cord to keep the appliances running or will you have to make other arrangements for your perishable foods?

There is much more to major remodeling jobs than what first meets the eye. Look ahead, plan carefully, and be prepared for unexpected changes in your plans. If you do this, you will avoid many problems and be better prepared for trouble that cannot be dodged.

SETTING A REALISTIC TIMETABLE

Another part of your planning should include setting a realistic timetable for the completion of your job. This is often easier said than done. Remodeling jobs rarely go as planned, and staying on schedule can be very difficult. If one aspect of the job gets out of sync, the whole job can be affected. For example, if the kitchen countertop is not delivered on time, the plumber will not be able to install the kitchen sink, garbage disposer, or dishwasher. The delay in installing the disposer and dishwasher will throw off the electrician's schedule, and the chain of events can go on and on. If the cabinet delivery is delayed, the whole job can come to a halt.

Meeting deadlines on a production schedule can be achieved if the deadlines are realistic. If you allow adequate time for each phase of work, the chances are good that you can meet your self-imposed deadlines. There will, of course, be times when you can't control delays. Invariably, some jobs are plagued with bad luck: the wrong cabinets will be shipped; the sink will be damaged; the painter won't show up for days, and so on. Is it bad luck or bad planning? Usually it is a deficiency in organizational skills and follow-up effort, but there are times when the best efforts cannot alleviate the problems.

How Can You Set Realistic Time Goals?

How can you set realistic time goals? If you are hiring contractors to do your job, ask them how long their portions of the job will take. Consult cost-estimating manuals that give estimates for the time needed to complete various phases of work. Compare the data in the estimating manual with the answers given by your contractors. If the two estimates are similar, you should be right on track. When the time estimates differ substantially, investigate further. For example, if you are examining three electrical bids and one electrician says the job will take two days, ask the other electricians how long they believe the work will take. Once you have their time projections you can begin to answer your question about the time required to complete the electrical phase of the job.

A form can be used to list each phase of work to be done and the estimated time allowed for the work. If you are going to do the work yourself, setting a completion date will be a little more difficult. You can still use cost-estimating manuals to help determine your time needs. Many of these guides list the number of hours a job should take to complete when professionals are doing the work. Some of the guides give advice on how to adjust the time estimates to allow for a lack of professional experience.

Remodeling jobs almost always take longer to complete than anyone except seasoned remodelers expect. Once you have outlined a production schedule, build in some extra time for unexpected work and delays. For example, when you remove the floor covering in your bathroom, you may find that the subfloor and floor joists have been damaged by a water leak at the base of the toilet. This type of unexpected work will increase the cost of your job and the time it takes to complete it. By building in a buffer for unexpected problems and mistakes in time estimates, you will be more likely to finish on or ahead of schedule.

There are many circumstances that no individual can control fully, and this is why organizing a completion schedule that will work is not easy. The best you can do is to create a schedule and work hard to maintain it. This may mean hounding contractors or suppliers to do what they have promised, but in all cases staying on schedule will take effort. Jobs don't run themselves. If they did, there would be no need for general contractors.

CONTRACTOR CONSIDERATIONS

Contractor considerations may also play a significant role in the success of your remodeling project. Choosing the right contractors is not always easy, but it is necessary. The wrong contractors can turn your remodeling dream into a nightmare. Here are some tips for hiring contractors:

- Any contractor you hire should be properly licensed and insured.

- You may find it beneficial to work with bonded contractors.

- Don't take chances with part-timers who are not licensed or insured.

- Make sure your contractors obtain all needed permits and inspections.

- If you are going to hire contractors, choose them carefully.

- Check the references of potential contractors.

While you cannot control all aspects of your job, there is much you can do to keep it on schedule. For example, if you inspect all materials as soon as they are delivered, you can avoid some loss of time.

CONTRACTOR QUESTIONNAIRE

PLEASE ANSWER ALL THE FOLLOWING QUESTIONS, AND EXPLAIN ANY "NO" ANSWERS.

Company name _____

Physical company address _____

Company mailing address _____

Company phone number _____

After hours phone number _____

Company President/Owner _____

President/Owner address _____

President/Owner phone number _____

How long has company been in business? _____

Name of insurance company _____

Insurance company phone number _____

Does company have liability insurance? _____

Amount of liability insurance coverage _____

Does company have Workman's Comp. insurance? _____

Type of work company is licensed to do _____

List Business or other license numbers _____

Where are licenses held? _____

If applicable, are all workman licensed? _____

Are there any lawsuits pending against the company? _____

Has the company ever been sued? _____

Does the company use subcontractors? _____

Is the company bonded? _____

Who is the company bonded with? _____

Has the company ever had complaints filed against it? _____

Are there any judgments against the company? _____

Please list 3 references of work similar to ours:

#1 _____

#2 _____

#3 _____

Please list 3 credit references:

#1 _____

#2 _____

#3 _____

Please list 3 trade references:

#1 _____

#2 _____

#3 _____

Please note any information you feel will influence our decision:

_____

ALL OF THE ABOVE INFORMATION IS TRUE AND ACCURATE AS OF THIS DATE.

DATE:_____   COMPANY NAME: _____

BY:_____ TITLE: _____

Figure 1.5   Example of a questionnaire for a contractor.

MATERIAL ORDER LOG

SUPPLIER: _____

_____

_____

DATE ORDER WAS PLACED: _____

TIME ORDER WAS PLACED: _____

NAME OF PERSON TAKING ORDER: _____

PROMISED DELIVERY DATE: _____

ORDER NUMBER: _____

QUOTED PRICE: _____

_____

_____

DATE OF FOLLOW-UP CALL: _____

MANAGER'S NAME: _____

TIME OF CALL TO MANAGER: _____

MANAGER CONFIRMED DELIVERY DATE: _____

MANAGER CONFIRMED PRICE: _____

NOTES AND COMMENTS

_____

_____

_____

_____

_____

_____

_____

_____

_____

_____

_____

_____

Figure 1.6   Example of a material order log.

- Check with local agencies that report complaints against contractors.

- Don't give contractors large deposits for the work to be done.

THE END RESULT

Knowing what you want the end result of your remodeling to be is also important. Are you doing the job to build equity in your home or to satisfy your personal preferences? It is possible to do both at the same time, but the two don't necessarily go hand in hand. If you are hoping to build equity in your home through the remodeling of a kitchen, you must be selective in the work you do.

Spending too much on improvements can negate any equity you hoped to build. On the other hand, if you are making the changes to suit your personal desires and you are not worried about recovering your investment, as long as you can pay for it, you can do it.

Take some time to decide what you hope to gain from your remodeling and ask yourself some questions, such as:

- Do you want more light in your kitchen?

- How much cabinet or counter space to you want?

- Will doing the work yourself and building several thousand dollars of equity in your home make you happy?

These are the types of questions to ask yourself. Allow adequate time to find the real reasons for your urge to remodel. If you dedicate enough time to the planning of your project, you are much more likely to wind up with results that will please you.

2

Drawing Your Own Rough Plans

When you are planning a remodeling job, sketching your intentions is a good way to design a rough plan of action. Having a sketch of what your want to do will make planning the job much easier, and you don't have to be an architect to draw your own preliminary plans.

Line drawings are often very effective for interior remodeling jobs. If you are not making structural changes in your home, a simple line drawing may be all you need to get the job done. Even if you have no artistic ability or inclination, you can do a pretty fair job of sketching a rough plan with the help of a ruler and some graph paper.

If your job is complex enough to warrant elements such as cross-sections and elevations that you are unable to draw, there are many options for you to consider. Architects are one option, but plans drawn by architects are usually very expensive, and this can be cost-prohibitive in many remodeling jobs.

Let's imagine that we are going to remodel a kitchen but are not sure what we want it to look like. Where should we start our planning? It would be nice if we could look through a book of floor plans, but finding a book that contains only kitchen plans is not easy. There are, however, many books available that contain house plans and these books can be a good starting point.

BOOKS WITH HOUSE PLANS

Books with house plans also contain kitchen plans. The plans are not drawn individually. They are a part of the overall house plan, but that's all right. In the planning stage of a remodeling job, you are likely to be looking for ideas, and these books of plans can give your enough ideas to keep you busy all winter. Soon your problem will not be coming up with ideas, it will be deciding on which ideas to incorporate into your personal plans.

A single book of house plans may very well contain over a hundred different kitchen layouts. When you consider how many different books of plans are available, you might find thousands of designs to work with. Many of the designs will be similar, but each will have its own special features. You can borrow from several plans to come up with an ideal plan for your house.

House plans on the Internet are a good source of ideas for the remodeling of your kitchen.

When you look at the floor plans for various kitchens, notice how simple they are. Most of them will consist only of simple lines. Some may be drawn in a dimensional perspective, but most will just be simple line drawings. Don't you think you could draw similar plans with the help of a few drafting tools and some graph paper?

SKETCHING YOUR OWN PLANS

Sketching your own plans can be very simple. If you gather a few basic drafting instruments, you can make the drawings look like those in the books of plans. There are templates

Figure 2.1   This beautiful kitchen is the end result of careful design. *Courtesy of Wellborn Cabinet, Inc.*

available that enable you to draw sinks, appliances, and doors with ease. All you have to do is follow the stencil and you can't go wrong. An architectural-scale ruler is not too expensive, and it makes scaling a drawing very easy. If you don't want to buy a scale rule, you can use any ruler to create your own scale drawing. The grids on graph paper make scaling a rough drawing possible for anyone. The point is that you can draw your own preliminary plans.

> Many software manufacturers sell consumer-grade drafting programs for computer-aided drafting. These programs are available on the Internet, in computer stores, and in large chain stores. Prices for these programs are often less than $50.

Templates

Inexpensive templates are available for every symbol you see on an average floor plan. Some of these symbols represent the following:

- Windows
- Doors
- Sinks
- Appliances
- Cabinets
- Other items

All of these items can be drawn with plastic guides. All you have to do is hold the template on the paper and trace a pencil around the stencils. Your results should look as good as those of a professional.

Scale Rulers

Scale rulers don't cost much, but they make drawing scaled drawings much easier than it would be with a standard ruler. If you want one of these devices, get an architectural-scale ruler. It will be of the most use to you for construction blueprints.

Scale rulers are equipped to handle several different scales. It won't matter whether you are working with a $\frac{1}{4}$-inch scale or a $\frac{1}{2}$-inch scale; your scale ruler will convert the scale to real-world measurements. All you do is position the ruler on a line and measure it. If you are working with a $\frac{1}{4}$-inch scale, a 3-inch line will read as 12 feet on the scale ruler.

Regular rulers can be used to work with scale drawings, but you will have to do the math conversions on your own. This not only consumes more time, but it also makes mistakes more likely.

Graph Paper

Graph paper is the best type of paper to use for your preliminary drawing. The paper has grids spaced at proportional distances. You can assign each of these grids a distance value. For example, you might say the distance between horizontal lines equals 1 foot or 1 inch, depending on what you are drawing.

Once you have graph paper, a ruler, and a pencil, you can draw a rough plan of what you want to do. Having a template for your symbols will make the drawing look more professional, but you can get by without the template. Equipped with these tools, it takes almost no artistic ability to draw a simple floor plan.

> Draw all your plans to scale. I can remember numerous jobs where customers had wonderful designs that simply would not work since the drawings were not to scale. It's easy to get a double-door refrigerator between a cabinet and a wall if you don't scale the drawing, but when it comes time for the real installation, the appliance may not fit.

GETTING PROFESSIONAL HELP

Getting professional help with your working drawings is not difficult, but it can be expensive. Architects are very well qualified for drawing your plans, but their fees are generally cost-prohibitive for simple home remodeling. Who can you turn to if you don't want to pay the price for an architect? You could check into drafting companies.

Drafting Firms

Many drafting firms draw blueprints and floor plans. Again, if you only need a floor plan, you can do it yourself. But if you are doing extensive work or structural work, you would be better off with professionally drawn plans. Most drafting companies will draw working plans from your rough drawing for very reasonable prices.

Free Drafting Services

There is another option that may not cost you anything. Some building-supply stores will provide free drafting services for their customers. If you are willing

> College students are another possible source for low-cost plans. Students who are taking drafting classes may have the ability to give you good working plans for a low price.

to buy your materials from the supplier, there is a good chance that you can get your plans drawn for free or for a very modest fee. However, the free plans may not be the bargain they appear to be. Before you commit to a deal, check the supplier's prices and the quality of the materials. It is possible that the price you will pay for the materials is far too much. If this is the case, you may be better off to pay someone else to draw your plans so you can buy your materials wherever you want.

HOW ACCURATE DO PRELIMINARY SKETCHES HAVE TO BE?

How accurate do preliminary sketches have to be? There is no rule that says preliminary sketches must be to scale, but if they are not, it is easy to lose perspective on the job. It is not important for the symbols to be exact drafting symbols, but you should strive to maintain a consistent scale, regardless of what the scale is.

If you draw the floor plan without using a scale, objects may appear much larger or smaller than they actually are. Many homeowners sit down with pencil and paper and draw a kitchen plan that looks spacious, but if the sketch is not drawn to scale, there is no way to judge how spacious the room will be. If you are freehand-drawing a kitchen cabinet, it is easy to draw it to fit any space you want. Many homeowners fail to realize how large kitchen components are. This distorts the options available in a given space. To avoid disappointment when the construction starts, draw your sketches to scale.

JUDGING SIZES

Judging sizes for some items can be difficult for homeowners. Take a look at the questions and answers below to get a feel of the types of sizes that you may need to deal with:

- Q: Do you know how wide a typical base cabinet for a kitchen sink is?
- A: It is normally 5 feet wide.

- Q: What are standard widths for wall cabinets that are not custom-made?

- A: The most common widths for stock wall cabinets are 12, 15, 18, 24, 30, and 36 inches.

- Q: How deep are most of these cabinets?

- A: The depth of most wall cabinets is 30 inches.

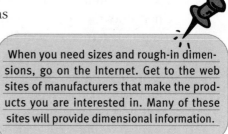

When you need sizes and rough-in dimensions, go on the Internet. Get to the web sites of manufacturers that make the products you are interested in. Many of these sites will provide dimensional information.

Knowing these typical sizes will be important when designing your new kitchen.

How will you know what sizes to use for various items? You can look in catalogs for sizes, or you could go to building-supply centers and measure various items. Sizes are easy to come by.

Figure 2.2   Dimensions of various cabinets. *Courtesy of Wellborn Cabinet, Inc.*

CODE REQUIREMENTS

Code requirements are another factor that you must consider when drawing your working plans. If you are only drawing a rough sketch and will have a professional prepare your working plans, you can get by without knowing code requirements. The professional will adjust your drawing to comply with them.

If you draw your own working plans and submit them for approval to the local code-enforcement office, the code officer will let you know if the drawing is in violation of the code. Door widths, ceiling heights, electrical outlets, and plumbing fixtures are where most of the spacing requirements will be scrutinized.

Once you have completed your preliminary plans, there are likely to be many changes made to them. It is best to make these changes before work is begun, but that is not always possible. While it is probable that there will be changes made after the job is started, it is best to firm up the plans as much as possible before starting work.

EXTENSIVE REMODELING

If you are planning an extensive remodeling job, you will benefit from having a good understanding of blueprints and design plans. While complex drawings are rarely used in minor remodeling jobs, they are common when doing larger jobs. For example, if you are expanding your kitchen and relocating your fixtures, appliances, and cabinets, you should have a detailed set of plans to work from. The need for solid working plans is essential if you want contractors to do the job the way you envision it.

It is easy for two people to see the same vision in a different light. For example, assume that you tell your plumber that you want an almond-colored, enameled cast-iron sink. This seems like a clear description, doesn't it? Okay, now assume that you leave for work, and when you get home, the plumber has installed an almond-colored, composite sink. You take one look at it and hate it. The sink is not close to what you wanted, except in its color. What are you going to do?

You see, many contractors use what they are able to get and hope that homeowners will accept them. You don't have to. If you had given the plumber a make and model number to work with, you would have the sink you wanted. As it is, you have a sink you don't want. This is why detailed specifications are needed on all jobs.

> Many homeowners opt to save a few hundred dollars by not having professional blueprints prepared for their remodeling jobs. Sometimes these homeowners are able to communicate what they want to contractors and get it. But many times communication between the parties leaves something to be desired, and the job does not turn out as the homeowners had hoped.

> If you are doing a major remodel, plans and specifications should be considered a compulsory expense. The money or time you spend in preparing precise plans and specifications can save you time, money, and aggravation.

HOW WILL BLUEPRINTS HELP YOUR JOB?

How will blueprints help your job? Blueprints will act as a road map for all work being done. Let's say that you are remodeling your kitchen and an island cabinet will be installed. The island will hold a vented indoor grill and will be a focal point of your kitchen.

Assume that you are doing this job without the aid of blueprints. Before leaving for work, you point with your finger to a place where you want the carpenters to install your island. You talk with your carpenters, electricians, and appliance people and feel you have the installation of the island and grill well defined. Then you leave for work.

When you return home that evening, your island and grill are installed, but what have those idiots done? The doors on the island cabinet are on the wrong side, and the grill is sitting

Figure 2.3 This unique design requires good communication with the contractor. *Courtesy of Armstrong*

in the top backwards—at least that's the way you see it. The island is where you told the workers to put it. It just is not facing the direction you thought it would. You knew which way you wanted everything installed, but you failed to tell the contractors anything more than where on the floor to place the unit.

There are many times when detailed drawings can be avoided, but you should never hire contractors to do a job without explicit specifications.

Since the unit is installed permanently, it will be expensive to have its location altered. The job would involve ductwork, electrical work, and carpentry work. You can't expect the contractors to perform the work free of charge, but the work must be done to get the island the way you want it. This means that your budget has just been overrun because of poor communication. A detailed set of blueprints would have prevented this problem. When do you need blueprints? Blueprints, or at least line drawings, are beneficial on all jobs, but they are a near necessity for large jobs.

Kitchen Expansion

Kitchen expansion is one form of remodeling that should be done with the help of good blueprints or line drawings. This type of work involves many changes and opportunities for confusion. If you are building an addition on your home to expand the kitchen, blueprints become even more important.

When you are changing fixture locations, cabinet locations, wall locations, and so forth, detailed plans should be used. Basically, unless the job is so obvious that no one could make a mistake, plans should be used.

Many code-enforcement offices will not issue permits for work to be done until they are provided with plans and specifications. So even if you don't want a set of plans, you may have to have them drawn in order to obtain the necessary permits.

READING BLUEPRINTS

Reading blueprints is not difficult if you take your time and understand the symbols used on the drawings. In the case of most kitchen remodeling jobs, the blueprints will not be very complicated. However, it will still be necessary to understand how plans are drawn to scale and what the various symbols mean.

If you are working from a set of professionally drawn blueprints, everything you need to know to read them is likely to be included on the plans. There should be notes that indicate the scale used on the plans, and there should be a section that shows all the symbols and their meanings. This is called a legend.

Learning what the symbols and different types of lines represent is not difficult. Working with scaled drawings is easiest when you have a scale ruler, but any ruler will do. Most blueprints are drawn with a scale in which ¼ inch on the blueprint is equal to one foot in real life. In other words, a countertop that measures two inches on this type of blueprint would actually be eight feet long.

It is important to note that not all blueprints are drawn to the same scale. In fact, it is possible for the scale to change from one page of the prints to the next. The scale often changes for cross-section details and elevations. Before relying on scale measurements, check each section of the plans for the scale being used.

If you are doing the work yourself, professionally drawn blueprints will be your guide. By checking the prints, you can see what size lumber is required, how thick the countertop should be, how far below the ceiling the cabinets should hang, and where your fixtures should be placed. A good set of blueprints will leave nothing to the imagination.

SPECIFICATIONS

We have already seen some examples of how specifications can influence the progress of a job. If you are working as a do-it-yourselfer, professionally prepared specifications can answer many of your questions. While you may know that an underlayment is needed for your new tile floor, you may not know what size or type to use. Professional specifications will tell you what to use in all your remodeling tasks.

If you are thinking that you don't need clear specifications when doing the work yourself, you are likely to be wrong. Even professional tradespeople rely on specifications drafted by architects and engineers. It is one thing to know how to install a floor joist and quite another thing to know which size joist to install. Every job benefits from clear specifications, regardless of who is doing the work.

If you provide a carpenter with a detailed set of plans and specifications and the job doesn't turn out right, you have grounds for insisting that changes be made, at no cost to you, to bring the job into compliance with the plans and specifications. You should have all contractors sign a copy of the plans and specifications to prove that they were

When you hire others to do remodeling for you, detailed specifications are the only way to ensure that the job will be done the way you want it done.

given a set. This can be of great benefit if you are one of the unfortunate few who winds up in court with a cantankerous contractor.

THE KEY TO UNDERSTANDING BLUEPRINTS AND DESIGN PLANS

The key to understanding blueprints and design plans is patience. Take your time in looking the plans over and familiarize yourself with the symbols and scales. Practice scaling distances on lines where the distances are given. If you see a wall with a noted length of 8 feet, scale it and see if you come up with the right measurement. Always confirm the scale on the section of drawing that you are working with. Look at the legend of symbols and search the plans until you can find and identify each one. Practice does make perfect when it comes to reading blueprints.

3

Solidifying Plans and Estimating Job Costs

Solidifying your plans before beginning any remodeling work will save time and money. Remodeling is known for its unexpected changes in plans, but you should do your best to avoid in-progress changes. Even after doing your best you will probably experience some problems. Professional remodelers have problems with most jobs, so it is unlikely that you will avoid them. However, you can hedge your odds.

What can you do to solidify your plans? There are many ways to reduce the risks of on-the-job problems. If you will be using contractors on your job, you should meet with each of them prior to starting work. One common problem on many jobs is conflict between the different trades. It is not unusual for plumbers and heating mechanics to get in each other's way. Electricians sometimes block the paths of other trades, and painters and drywall finishers often argue about who is at fault for less-than-perfect wall finishes. Of course, if you are doing all the work yourself, there won't be anyone else to worry about. All you will have to do is stay out of your own way.

Most homeowners don't possess all the skills necessary to do a full-scale remodeling job without some professional help. However, any homeowner can gain enough knowledge to act as a general contractor, and this effort can save a considerable amount of money on the cost of a job. Just by acting as your own general contractor you can save between 10 and 30 percent on the retail price of a job. On a $20,000 kitchen-remodeling job, this can amount to some serious money.

The minute you decide to involve other people in your job, you must make a commitment to refine your plans and specifications before starting any work. To show the importance of solid plans, let's look at a sample job and how it might be affected by a lack of proper preparation.

A MAJOR KITCHEN REMODEL

A major kitchen remodel can be a big undertaking. The work required in this type of job can involve a multitude of trades. What trades are likely to be involved? The work may involve any of the following:

- Demolition
- Rough carpentry
- Trim carpentry
- Plumbing
- Electrical
- Heating
- Drywall installation
- Drywall finishing
- Painting
- Floor covering
- Insulation installation
- Tile installation

Figure 3.1 Such an extreme change, such as this exotic kitchen design, is possible without much impact on existing systems. *Courtesy of Armstrong*

- Cabinet installation
- Other types of work

Can you do all these jobs? If you can, you are one of only a few homeowners who can handle this type of job without professional help.

Since many homeowners will not feel comfortable doing any of their own work, let's look at this job through the eyes of a person who is acting as a general contractor. If you plan to do portions of your own work, you can substitute your labor for the trades you are comfortable doing. Let's start the job from the beginning and see what problems might arise.

The first step will be to rip out the existing fixtures, cabinets, and floor covering. This phase of the job doesn't require a lot of skill, but you must be careful not to damage primary systems. For example, you have to cut the water off to the plumbing fixtures before removing them, and caution must be exercised when removing light fixtures.

Once the rip-out is complete, you must get rid of the debris. Here are some questions to ask yourself at this phase of the job:

- Have you made plans for having the debris removed? If you haven't, this is your first problem.

- Should you have arranged for a temporary trash receptacle to place the debris in to be hauled away at a later date?

- Should you have laid the debris on a tarp in your yard and scheduled someone to pick it up and dispose of it?

- Can you haul the debris to a dump area yourself?

Don't wait until you have debris to figure this out. Make a plan in advance. The removal of debris can require time to arrange, so it is important to take care of this before demolition work is started.

Considerable dust can infiltrate a home during the demolition phase of a remodeling job. Plan on sealing off the work area with plastic to contain the dust. Use masking tape to secure the plastic to door openings and weight the bottom of the plastic with a piece of wood to allow ingress and egress to the work area.

What will you do now that the rip-out is complete? Normally, any needed alterations to the heating or plumbing systems will be done first. It is unlikely that there would be a conflict between these two phases in an average kitchen-remodeling job.

After the plumbing and heating rough-ins are done, the electrical work is next. Again, in a typical kitchen remodel, this shouldn't cause any conflict. However, if you are expanding the size of the kitchen, the plumbers, electricians, and heating mechanics might all get in one another's way.

When all the rough-ins are complete and inspected by the local code officer, you are ready for the insulation installation. There may be no need for additional insulation in an interior-remodeling job. After any required insulation work and inspections, you are ready to hang drywall. This phase of the job should go smoothly. After the drywall is hung, you are ready to tape and finish it. This is a dusty job and it takes some special skills, but there should not be any special problems with this phase of the job.

Now you are ready for paint. What happens when the paint is applied and the finish of the walls is not acceptable? Is it the drywall contractor's fault or the painter's fault? This is a debate that can rage back and forth for what seems an eternity. There is one way to solve this problem, but you must plan for it in advance.

> Most rough-in work for the mechanical trades, which include plumbing, heating, and electrical work, requires an inspection from the local code-enforcement officer before the work is concealed. Don't allow this work to be hidden by insulation or wall coverings until you have proof of approved inspections.

Insist that the drywall contractor apply a coat of primer to the walls before leaving the job. When the primer is applied, any defects in the finish work will show up. This pins the fault on the right party. If the walls pass the primer test, you can move on to the painter. If the walls don't look good after the painting, you can hold the painter responsible. After the paint is done, you are ready to install the flooring. It is not unusual for the flooring contractor to mar the finish of new walls, so watch this phase closely.

> Some jurisdictions require insulation to be inspected prior to concealing it.

After the flooring is in, you are ready for the plumber to set fixtures. Then the heating mechanic can trim out the heating system and the electrician can finish the electrical work.

Trim carpentry can be done anytime after the finish flooring is in place, but it is often scheduled after the mechanical trades are complete.

When everything else is done, the painting contractor will probably have to come back to paint the trim and touch up any places blemished by the other trades.

When all the work is finished and inspected by the code officers, all that is left is the cleanup work. Once the cleaning is done, you have a fresh, revitalized kitchen. This doesn't sound too hard, does it? Well, it is not always as easy as it sounds. What could go wrong? Lots of problems could come up.

Insist that the drywall contractor apply a coat of primer to the walls before leaving the job. When the primer is applied, any defects in the finish work will show up.

Suppose your flooring contractor doesn't show up when scheduled—what will that affect? It will affect your entire finish schedule. For example, you wouldn't want the plumber to install the sink before the countertop goes in. This is a stupid thing to say, but it sets the bar. You have to look ahead. If something is wrong, you may have to reschedule all the trades that follow the flooring.

What would happen if one of the trades didn't pass the rough-in inspection? This problem could prohibit you from moving ahead with the drywall installation. If you have to postpone the drywall, the whole job slows down.

Avoid sending multiple trades into the job on the same day. If you have more than one trade on the job at a time, you will not know whom to blame for damages that occur.

The list of potential problems could go on and on, but you should be getting the idea that loose ends can affect your production schedule. These risks escalate when the size of the job is larger, as with major kitchen remodeling.

HOW CAN YOU AVOID ON-THE-JOB PROBLEMS?

How can you avoid on-the-job-problems? How you avoid problems will depend largely on the type of job you are doing and the number of people involved. To illustrate this, review the following list of problems and solutions:

- The first step is to have all agreements between you and your contractors in writing. The value of well-written contracts is immense. A good contract can protect you and your home while giving you control over the contractors.

- Open communication between the trades is also instrumental in the completion of a successful job. Having everyone who will be involved on the project get together on the job before work is started can help to eliminate confusion and conflicts before they affect your production schedule.

- Material deliveries are a frequent source of on-the-job problems. It is not uncommon for deliveries to arrive days after they were scheduled to appear on the job. If you have a place to store materials, order early and check each delivery carefully.

- If you make any changes in your plans or specifications after the job is started, make sure that all trades are aware of the changes.

A smooth remodeling job requires good organizational skills and a team effort. If everyone is working individually, oblivious to what others are doing, problems are sure to arise.

SOLID PLANS MAKE FOR SMOOTH JOBS

Solid plans make for smooth jobs. There will more than likely be some changes you cannot predict until the job is started, but make an effort to get all changes made before the work is in progress. No one likes to see a job lose its momentum. You will be stuck with a job that drags on and on, and the contractors who bid the job for a flat-rate fee will lose money.

Whenever there is a change in your plans or specifications, insist on written change orders that formalize the proposed changes. Get it in writing!

I cannot stress enough how important preplanning is for a successful remodeling job. If you plan well in advance and remain organized at all times, you can handle the unexpected much better than many professional contractors do.

ESTIMATING YOUR COSTS

Estimating your costs for a big remodeling job may seem like a formidable task, but it doesn't have to be. Cost estimating is a vital part of any remodeling job, and it is a job in itself. There are people who get paid good salaries for doing nothing but cost estimating. With today's technology, many professionals rely on computers and software for their estimating needs. While it is unlikely that you have access to high-tech estimating programs, you needn't feel helpless. There are many effective ways for you to develop accurate estimates for your labor and material needs.

If you have the skills to do all your own work, estimating your costs will be a little easier. All you will have to be concerned with are the prices for your materials. However, if you are an average homeowner, you will have to rely on some professional help to realize your remodeling goal. This will necessitate estimating the cost for those professional fees.

Since most homeowners need professional help, we will explore the ways to estimate both material prices and professional labor costs. While any one of the methods can produce an accurate estimate, you should combine the methods to assure the most accuracy in your estimates.

ESTIMATING WITH THE HELP OF CONTRACTORS

Estimating with the help of contractors is the easiest way to figure the cost of your job. Essentially, all you have to do is to ask several contractors to give you bids for the job. The contractors will be glad to give you estimates or quotes for the price of labor and materials to complete your project. This is a simple process, but there are some aspects of this type of estimating that can skew the numbers. If you want accurate figures, you should follow some basic rules. What are those rules? Let's find out.

Plans

If you are going to allow contractors to do your job for you, a set of plans for what you want done is an absolute necessity. Even if the job is a small one, you will want to give each contractor bidding the work a set of plans. Without the plans the contractors cannot possibly bid the job competitively.

The plans you issue to contractors don't have to be elaborate, but they must detail all important aspects of the job. A rough sketch of what you want done will probably be adequate, but don't attempt to estimate your job with contractors until you have some type of plans to hand out.

Specifications

Specifications are as important, if not more important, than plans when working with contractors. When you put your job out to bids, you want all contractors pricing the same

> Many contractors use the phrase "or equal" to build in flexibility for substitutions. Don't allow such a clause in your quotes or contracts. To obtain accurate estimates, you must be certain all contractors are bidding the job identically.

materials and services. This is only possible with a set of plans and a detailed set of specifications.

It is not enough to list your specifications casually. You should not say that you want a new sink, a new dishwasher, and new faucets. The specifications should include all technical data needed to identify the specific items you want. This information will normally include a model number, style, color, and similar information.

Substitutions

Sometimes contractors make substitutions in materials when bidding work. If you allow this to happen, it will be impossible to compare the bids you receive accurately. Many contractors use the phrase "or equal" to build in flexibility for substitutions. Don't allow such a clause in your quotes or contracts. To obtain accurate estimates, you must be certain all contractors are bidding the job identically.

Cost Projections

Item/Phase	Labor	Material	Total
Plans			
Specifications			
Permits			
Trash container deposit			
Trash container delivery			
Demolition			
Dump fees			
Rough plumbing			
Rough electrical			
Rough heating/ac			
Subfloor			
Insulation			
Drywall			
Ceramic tile			
Linen closet			
Baseboard trim			
Window trim			
Door trim			
Paint/wallpaper			
Underlayment			
Finish floor covering			
Linen closet shelves			
Closet door & hardware			
Main door hardware			
Wall cabinets			
Base cabinets			
Countertops			
Plumbing fixtures			
Trim plumbing material			
Final plumbing			
Shower enclosure			
Subtotal			

Figure 3.2   Example of a cost projections form.

Item/Phase	Labor	Material	Total
Light fixtures			
Trim electrical material			
Final electrical			
Trim heating/ac material			
Final heating/ac			
Bathroom accessories			
Clean up			
Trash container removal			
Window treatments			
Personal touches			
Financing expenses			
Miscellaneous expenses			
Unexpected expenses			
Margin of error			
Subtotal from first page			
Total estimated expense			

Figure 3.2 (*continued*)   Example of a cost projections form.

Contractor's Qualifications

A contractor's qualifications may affect the price you are quoted for a job. When you are working towards a final decision on which contractor to select and which price is right, you should consider the contractor's qualifications.

A building contractor who normally builds new houses may not be well qualified to give accurate price estimates for kitchen remodeling. While this contractor may be very familiar with what it costs to build a house, remodeling a kitchen may present circumstances that the builder is not experienced with in terms of pricing.

> When you are working towards a final decision on which contractor to select and which price is right, you should consider the contractor's qualifications.

A remodeling contractor who has not been in business long may not have the ability to produce accurate quotes. Some contractors will give a low price to get the work, but will they be around to finish the job? There are many situations in

Option	Vendor	L/M	Price	Notes
Solid trim				
Stained trim				
Solid doors				
Stained doors				
Valance over kitchen cabinets				
Dishwasher				
Garbage disposer				
Automatic garage door				
Opener				
Tile work				
Wood floors				
Fancy handrails				
Wood stairs				
Security system				
Cable television pre-wire				
Telephone pre-wire				
Intercom				
Additional oil tank				
Additional attic/crawl lighting				
Ground cover in crawl				
Mirrors				
Plywood instead of wafer board				
2 layers of subfloor or ¾ T & G				
Insulated wall sheathing				
Ridge vent				
Soffit vents				

Figure 3.3   Example of an estimating form for options

Option	Vendor	L/M	Price	Notes
Gutters	_____	____	____	____
Rain diverters	_____	____	____	____
Shutters	_____	____	____	____
Window screens	_____	____	____	____
Garage	_____	____	____	____
Deck	_____	____	____	____
Fireplace	_____	____	____	____
Power venter	_____	____	____	____
Flue	_____	____	____	____
Domestic coil	_____	____	____	____
Hot-water tank	_____	____	____	____
Cleaning	_____	____	____	____
Trash removal	_____	____	____	____
Landscaping	_____	____	____	____
Walkways	_____	____	____	____
Porches	_____	____	____	____
Vented range hood	_____	____	____	____
Tub/shower doors	_____	____	____	____
Sump pump & piping	_____	____	____	____
Flood lights	_____	____	____	____
Ceiling lights	_____	____	____	____
Ceiling fans	_____	____	____	____
Overhead/underground electrical service	_____	____	____	____
Wall wrap	_____	____	____	____
Rigid foam insulation	_____	____	____	____

Figure 3.3 (*continued*)   Example of an estimating form for options

COST PROJECTIONS			
Item/Phase	Labor	Material	Total
Total estimated expense			

Figure 3.4   Example of a cost projections form.

which a contractor's qualifications could affect the pricing and service you receive.

If you don't take the contractor's qualifications into consideration, you may base your plans on a given price and find out that the estimated price is far too low. You can avoid this problem by obtaining numerous bids for the job and comparing them. If a few are extremely low, avoid those contractors.

> When requesting bids for remodeling work, always get at least three bids. Having five bids is a better strategy.

Time of Completion

The time of completion for a job can affect the price of the work. Some contractors will take a job at a lower price if they can use it as fill-in work. This allows the contractor to have something to work on when previously scheduled work does not go as planned. For example, if a contractor is scheduled to build a deck and it rains, what can be done to salvage the day? Since it is rarely productive to build decks in the rain, the contractor could come to your job and work inside.

If you are not in a hurry to get your job completed, this can be a good approach to take in getting a low price and a good job. However, if time is of the essence, as it usually is with kitchen remodeling, you will probably not be willing to allow the job to drag out for months. Before you accept what appears to be the best bid, establish the time of completion for your work.

Time of Day

What does the time of day have to do with your pricing estimates? It can have a lot to do with it. There are many licensed, insured, reputable contractors who work part-time. These contractors often have full-time jobs during the day and work their own business at night and on weekends. This group of contractors can offer attractive pricing.

BID ADDENDUM
REQUEST FOR SUBSTITUTIONS

CUSTOMER NAME: Mr. & Mrs. J. P. Homeowner

CUSTOMER ADDRESS: 192 Hometown Street

CUSTOMER CITY/STATE/ZIP: Yooho City, NA 93001

CUSTOMER PHONE NUMBER: (000) 756-3333

JOB LOCATION: Same

PLANS & SPECIFICATIONS DATED: June 10, 2004

BID REQUESTED FROM: Mid Range Suppliers

SUPPLIER ADDRESS: 42 Supplier Street

CONTACT PERSON: Liz Materialwoman, Manager

DATE: July 25, 2004

TYPE OF WORK: Remodeling

THE FOLLOWING ITEMS ARE BEING SUBSTITUTED FOR THE ITEMS
SPECIFIED IN THE ATTACHED PLANS AND SPECIFICATIONS:

Roof shingles-The brand specified is not readily available. Our
proposed substitute is product number 2246 form WXYZ company.
The type, color, and general characteristics are very similar.

Siding-The brand requested is not available through our
distribution network. It can be special ordered, but this requires
payment prior to order placement. A proposed substitute is
product number 4456 from ABEC company. The color and general
features are essentially the same as the requested siding.

_____   _____
Contractor   Date   Customer   Date

Figure 3.5   Example of a bid addendum request for substitutions.

If you don't mind having your nights and weekends interrupted with the inconveniences of remodeling, you can save some money by finding part-time contractors. However, if you don't want your hours off from work consumed with the noise, dust, and general commotion of remodeling, you will probably have to pay more for the work you want done. If you are shopping for the lowest price, find out why the lowest price is so low.

Quotes and Estimates

Do you know the difference between quotes and estimates? Estimates are just that, estimates. They don't guarantee a fixed price for a job. Since estimates are not quotes, it is hard to hold a contractor to an estimated price. When you are trying to estimate the cost of your remodeling project, you shouldn't base your figures on estimates provided by contractors. You need quotes.

Working with part-time contractors can be risky, but it can also be a great bargain. If the contractors are licensed and insured and can do the work within the time limits that you set, they could be a good deal. On the other hand, these contractors may not stay in business long enough to finish your job or to tend to any needed warranty work. You will have to decide between the risk and the reward.

Quotes are guaranteed prices that will not increase. They are usually good for thirty days. Once you make a commitment to sign a contract, the quoted price becomes the contract price and should not change. This is the only type of pricing that you can depend on.

Soft Costs

Soft costs are sometimes paid by contractors and sometimes paid by homeowners. When you are soliciting quotes for your job, you need to know if the quotes include all soft costs. What are soft costs? Soft costs are expenses such as permit fees, blueprints, and other fees that are not related directly to materials and labor. Before accepting any quote as the final figure for your job, identify all necessary soft costs and how they will be paid for.

MATERIAL TAKE-OFFS

What are material take-offs? They are simply lists of materials that will be needed to complete a job. If you plan to estimate your job without the help of contractors, it will be your responsibility to come up with a take-off of the materials you need. Why are these lists called take-offs? They are called take-offs because the lists are developed by taking material information off a set of plans. In other words, you would look at your plans and see that you need 120 square feet of underlayment to make a take-off for your kitchen floor.

Few homeowners will have the ability to make accurate take-offs from blueprints. For those homeowners working as do-it-yourselfers, this can be a problem. When you hire a plumber to replace the fixtures in your kitchen, you don't have to be concerned with how many compression ferrules or supply tubes will be needed. The plumber takes care of it for you. However, if you are going to replace your own fixtures, you will need to estimate the types and amounts of materials you will need. If you have never replaced plumbing fixtures before, you are likely to make mistakes in your estimates. Estimating the material needs for a complete kitchen remodel is much more difficult.

How will you make an accurate material take-off? You could guesstimate the needs for the job, but you will wind up with too many of some items and not enough of others. Since it is unlikely that you will be able to produce an accurate list of your needs from blueprints, the best option is to seek professional help.

What types of professionals will help you with your estimate for materials? If your plans were drawn by a professional, there is a good chance that that person will provide you with a list of materials needed to complete the work. You will have to pay for the information, but it should be accurate and the cost is not likely to break your budget.

Are there any options other than contractors and the professionals who draw plans for accurate take-offs? Yes—you can seek assistance from material suppliers. Almost any store that sells the supplies you need will be willing to help you establish a list of materials from your plans. Some places charge for this service and others provide it free of charge so long as you buy your materials from them. Material suppliers can be of great help in estimating your costs.

ESTIMATING WITH THE HELP OF MATERIAL SUPPLIERS

Estimating your costs with the help of material suppliers is a fine way to establish realistic cost projections for the materials needed in your job. Not all take-offs from suppliers will be as accurate as those provided by an architect, but they will be close enough for most needs.

To get a supplier to estimate your material needs and costs, all you have to do is provide a set of plans and specifications. Asking a supplier to bid your job from plans and specs will not necessarily give you a detailed take-off, but it will give you a fixed price to work with. You should get prices from several suppliers and compare them.

Ask the suppliers to break their prices down into phases of work. For example, ask that you be given separate prices for cabinets, countertops, flooring, framing lumber, and so on. If you have several material bids that are broken down this way, you can compare each phase to spot mistakes the suppliers may have made. For example, one supplier may list eight base cabinets where another supplier showed nine. At first you may not know which supplier's take-off is correct, but you will know that someone is wrong and that will enable you to establish your true needs.

Once you have obtained and reviewed several estimates for your materials, you will have a good idea as to what your costs will run. The other part of your job to estimate will be soft costs and labor. If you are doing the work yourself, estimating the cost of labor will not be important. The soft costs will probably include permit fees and working drawings, and you may not even need professionally drawn plans.

ESTIMATING WITH THE HELP OF COST-ESTIMATING GUIDES

Estimating with the help of cost-estimating guides is another way to project the expense of your job. With the use of these guides it is possible to predict the cost for both labor and materials. There are a number of cost-estimating guides available in bookstores, and most of them provide a lot of useful information.

There are drawbacks to depending on estimating books. These books can age and become out of date. Material prices can jump up and down frequently, and the books cannot foresee these changes. Since the books are written generically, the figures given may not be applicable in your particular situation.

Good estimating guides provide a way for you to convert generic estimates into regional estimates. Since prices in California are not the same as prices in Florida, the broad-brush estimates must be refined. Multipliers are normally used to factor in compensation for regional differences. These books can be very accurate, and they are an excellent way to evaluate prices given to you by suppliers and contractors.

If you plan to use cost-estimating guides, use them in conjunction with the other ways of estimating your costs. Don't depend on them exclusively.

My personal experience with cost-estimating manuals has shown that they usually predict estimates higher than most residential contractors give. I have figured jobs and then compared my figures with cost guides and found less than a $100 difference on big jobs. This is truly amazing. On the other hand, I have seen projections in guides for labor rates that were nearly double what most contractors were charging at the time in my area. I feel that the guides are useful, but I don't think you should rely on them as your sole source of information. If you are willing to spend the time to combine all these estimating methods, you can establish a very accurate estimate for the cost of your job.

4

Choosing Your
Materials

T he chore of selecting your materials can be a perplexing. It can also be a lot of fun. There are so many types of materials competing with each other in the field of remodeling that even professionals have trouble keeping up with what's available and what's best. For the average homeowner, trying to tell the difference between four different windows that look the same but have huge differences in cost can be all but impossible. The decision on whether to use wafer board or plywood for a subfloor can cause hours of troubled thought. Asking yourself which type of kitchen faucet will give the best service and appearance for the least amount of money can drive you crazy. All these questions and more can arise when you are trying to decide which materials to use. This chapter is going to show you some simple ways to sort through the maze of products available.

The proper selection of materials can save a lot of money on the overall cost of large remodeling jobs. There are some situations where buying the best materials available will pay off and other occasions

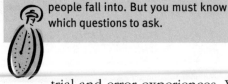

How can you, the homeowner, avoid costly mistakes? Research is the answer. If you ask enough questions and study enough product literature, you can avoid many pitfalls that people fall into. But you must know which questions to ask.

when less expensive materials will get the job done and save you money without sacrificing appearance or durability.

Knowing how to pick the proper materials is a skill remodelers often learn from trial-and-error experiences. While learning from experience is an effective method, it does get costly. And for homeowners it is unlikely that they will ever do enough remodeling to benefit from lessons learned the hard way.

SUBFLOORING

Subflooring is the flooring between the finished floor covering and the floor joists. The subflooring in most remodeling jobs does not need to be replaced, but there are times when it does. If the subflooring has been damaged by water or other causes, it may be necessary to replace it.

The three most common choices for subflooring material are plywood, wafer board, and a newer product that is much more resistant to water than either of the other options. This product goes by different brand names and comes in standard 4-x-8-foot sheets. If there will be only one layer of subflooring, the material should be of a tongue-and-groove (T & G) type. Some people install two layers of CDX plywood as subflooring, and others install one layer of tongue-and-groove plywood. If only one layer is being used, it is frequently ¾-inch T & G plywood. Most codes require this standard.

Wafer board is much less expensive than plywood—often half the cost. For this reason many professionals install a layer of wafer board and cover it with a thin layer of underlayment. By the time you add up the cost of the two layers and the time it takes to install them, one layer of T & G plywood is often less expensive. However, working with T & G materials in the

Figure 4.1 Selection of superior materials makes this kitchen both functional and striking. *Courtesy of Wellborn Cabinet, Inc.*

confined space of a kitchen can be troublesome. It is one thing to build a new house using T & G throughout and quite another to fit it into the tight spaces available in most remodeling jobs.

The water-resistant material is more expensive than plywood or wafer board, but I use it. The added protection against water problems is worth it to me, and the cost is not staggering. Talk to your contractor or supplier to see what brands of this type of material they recommend and have available.

Since kitchen remodeling does not require large quantities of subflooring, there will not be substantial money saved with any method or material. While installing two layers of subflooring may seem like twice as much work as installing one layer of T & G material, under remodeling conditions it is not. For most remodeling jobs it will be easier to install two layers of standard materials than one layer of T & G materials.

LUMBER

Lumber is available in different grades and at different prices. While the studs behind your walls won't be seen after the job is finished, their quality can affect the finished look of your project. Wood that twists and bends will warp the walls and can create defects in the finished wall surface. If you want to avoid problems with your lumber, insist on kiln-dried wood. For most applications a 2-grade lumber will be your best bet.

> If you have lumber delivered that will be kept outside, be sure to keep it dry. Letting rain get to your lumber can cause trouble down the road.

VINYL FLOORING

Vinyl flooring can range dramatically in price. The pricing spectrum may start at less than $13 per square yard and rise to a price in excess of $45 a square yard. An average grade of sheet vinyl flooring might be in the neighborhood of $18 per square yard.

> Vinyl flooring should be warm when it is installed. If you are doing a job during cold weather, be sure to bring the flooring in before you plan to install it so that it can warm up.

Cheap vinyl can be difficult to install because it is not as flexible as better grades. Inexpensive vinyl is not likely to wear well, and it is prone to more cuts and tears. Vinyl flooring priced between $18 and $23 per square yard should be relatively easy to install, and it should hold up well.

BASE CABINETS

Cabinets are one of the most expensive elements of kitchen remodeling, and base cabinets account for a big part of this expense. There are many types of cabinets to consider, some of which include:

Figure 4.2   Examples of vinyl flooring. *Courtesy of Armstrong*

- Sink bases
- Drawer bases
- Bases with doors
- Bases with turntables
- Bases with pull-out trash receptacles
- The list goes on

If this isn't enough to confuse you, these base cabinets are made from a myriad of materials.

Very few cabinets are made of solid wood. Most contain some composite materials. If you want cabinets that are true solid-wood cabinets, be prepared to spend plenty of money. Most cabinets will have solid-wood fronts and plywood or particleboard interiors.

When you buy cabinets, you will have to choose between dovetail joints and butt joints. Dovetail joints should last longer.

When you consider door options, you must decide if you want raised panels, flush doors, doors with finger pulls, or doors meant to accept hardware. This is a personal choice and shouldn't have a bearing on the durability of your job.

When checking out drawer bases, be sure to test how well the drawers slide in and out. Look for bases that have the drawers mounted on quality glides. This type of construction will provide years of trouble-free operation.

Investigate the structural integrity of the base cabinets. Good cabinets have supports in all corners, and the cabinets are firm. Cheap cabinets come in a you-assemble package with screws and little else. These units are the least desirable but also the least expensive.

Most people should avoid bargain cabinets that are sold unfinished. Finishing cabinets is not easy work, and it is easy to wind up with cabinets that don't match.

COUNTERTOPS

It is best not to purchase countertops until the base cabinets have been installed. This slows down the job, but it eliminates much of the risk of buying a countertop that doesn't fit. Countertops cannot usually be returned for credit, so it is important to get the right top on the first attempt.

If you are buying your cabinets and counters from a custom cabinet company, you will not have to worry about measurements. A representative will measure your kitchen and decide on the proper sizes. However, if you are dealing with a general supplier, you may have to measure for your own countertop. If this is the case, have the supplier explain to you exactly how to make the measurements for the type of top you are ordering.

Good, durable countertops are not terribly expensive, and they are available in a number of different colors and designs. Browsing through samples at your supplier will show you all the options. Expensive, specialty counters are not usually justified in average kitchens, but there are plenty of high-dollar tops available if you are so inclined.

WALL CABINETS

You can use the same basic rules applied to base cabinets for wall cabinets. Look for sturdy cabinets that offer a good appearance and adjustable shelves.

KITCHEN SINKS

Kitchen sinks can cost as little as $50 or more than $400. Most modern kitchens are equipped with double-bowl stainless-steel sinks. Some kitchens have enameled cast-iron sinks, and some sinks have single or double bowls with specialty bowls. A simple stainless-steel sink with two bowls is adequate for most kitchens.

While all stainless-steel sinks may look alike, there are differences. Some sinks are coated to reduce the noise made by water running into them. This sound-proofing costs extra and is not seen, but it may be worthwhile.

> The big difference between grades of stainless-steel sinks is the gauge of their metal. Some sinks are so flimsy that a garbage disposer will pull the bowl downward.

The big difference between grades of stainless-steel sinks is the gauge of their metal. Some sinks are so flimsy that a garbage disposer will pull the bowl downward. Look for a sink that does not dimple in and pop out when you press on the drain hole. For example, a 20-gauge sink is stronger than a 22-gauge sink.

LIGHT FIXTURES

Light fixtures are one type of material where you can spend a little or a lot and not really be able to see much difference. Recessed light fixtures can be bought for less than $40, but they are limited in the illumination they can provide.

Track lighting is very popular, and it can give plenty of illumination in different directions. Track lighting can be especially attractive and useful in a kitchen. Since track lighting is comprised of component parts, the price will vary with the style you select and the number of housings installed on the track. All in all, track lighting is a very affordable way to obtain good lighting.

Installing under-cabinet lighting is very popular in kitchens. You can use natural lighting with skylights, recessed lighting, ceiling fixtures, track lighting, or any other type of lighting that you like, but kitchens should have plenty of light.

WINDOWS

Windows can be especially bothersome to evaluate. There are so many types and styles of windows to consider that your mind can stay confused for days. To eliminate some of this confusion, you can read product literature. Let's look at some of the factors you may want to consider:

- The energy-efficiency of windows is rated in terms of U-value.

- The lower the U-value, the better and more efficient the window. For example, a window with a U-value of 4 would be more energy-efficient than a window with a U-value of 5.

- Casement windows are generally considered one of the most energy-efficient types of windows you can buy. They crank open and allow a full flow of ventilation when the glass is open.

Figure 4.3 Imagine the durability and beauty of this granite countertop and deep sink. *Photo courtesy of Moen, Inc.*

Figure 4.4 A vegetable sink, such as this, would be very handy to have in a kitchen. *Photo courtesy of Moen, Inc.*

Low-Profile Track

Low-Voltage Track Lights

Figure 4.5   Track lighting. *Courtesy of Nutone*

- Metal windows tend to sweat or condense. This moisture can cause damage to surrounding wood areas, and it is annoying visually.

- Wood windows provide good insulation and don't amplify sounds as much as metal windows do, but wood windows do require routine maintenance.

- Vinyl windows and vinyl-clad wood windows eliminate the need for painting. This maintenance-free feature is favored by many homeowners.

- Other options include gas-filled windows, low-E glass, glass that blocks UV rays, and so on.

- Garden windows are very popular in kitchens.

There are so many possibilities that you must study brochures from numerous manufacturers to determine which features are of importance to you.

TRIM MATERIALS

The trim materials you install in your project are going to be one of the features that will affect the finished look of your new kitchen. There are several choices available to you for trim. The two basic types of trim are finger-joint and clear. Finger-joint trim is less expensive than clear trim, but it is not suitable for staining. If you plan to paint your trim, finger-joint is fine. When you want to stain your trim wood, make sure it is clear trim or what is called stain-grade trim.

Colonial-style baseboards and casing are generally considered a good grade of standard trim. Clam-type baseboards are less expensive, but they are typically associated with lower-quality construction. You can use regular boards for trim. This is normally done when a rustic look is desired.

THE KEY TO CHOOSING THE RIGHT MATERIALS

The key to choosing the right materials is research. Educating yourself with product literature and books is an effective way to make sound purchasing decisions. If you don't understand what you are reading, ask professionals for their interpretations and opinions. If you allow adequate time for selecting your materials, you should be able to save money and still get good materials for your job.

5

Getting Your Best Price on Materials

S hopping for your best deal on materials will not be difficult once you know what you need and want. When you have a detailed list of material specifications, you can basically circulate the list among suppliers and wait for the best price. In theory, that's all there is to it. However, in real life, you will have to exert a little more energy to find the best bargains.

I had an occasion once to shop for materials with four different suppliers for the construction of a new house. I submitted identical plans and specifications to the suppliers and asked for detailed quotes. When all the quotes were in, there was a spread of about $4,000 from the lowest to the highest bid. This was many years ago when prices were much lower. Can you imagine that much difference among four suppliers for the same materials?

When I first saw the discrepancies I looked for errors in the bid sheets. I found none. After looking for mistakes, I began to compare the bids on an item-by-item basis. The picture started to come into focus as I studied the bid sheets. In some cases the materials I requested had been substituted, but for the most part, the difference was simply in the price of the materials. If this can happen to a professional contractor who buys materials on a daily basis, you can imagine how homeowners who may never visit a store again might be treated.

Aggressive shopping can save hundreds, or even thousands, of dollars on a kitchen remodeling job. There comes a point where running from store to store is not cost-effective, but sometimes it pays to deal with more than one supplier. Many people feel that they will get the best deal by purchasing all their materials from the same vendor; and while this should be true, it is not always the case. Let's look at some methods you can employ to get your best deal on materials.

Don't limit yourself to one supplier. Feel free to shop from many suppliers. It's okay to buy windows and doors from one supplier, lumber from another, and cabinets from yet another.

CIRCULATE YOUR PLANS AND SPECIFICATIONS

The first step in shopping prices is to circulate your plans and specifications. If you have a detailed take-off of the materials you want priced, that is all you need to distribute. Send the bid-request packages to several suppliers. If your job is a big one, it may pay to send bid packages to suppliers in other cities or states. It is amazing how much prices can differ from city to city and state to state.

If you do shop materials with long-distance suppliers, keep shipping costs in mind. They may outweigh any price advantage gained by buying at a distance. You may also want to consider the disadvantages long-distance suppliers offer in terms of product assistance and returns on damaged or improperly shipped items.

It is a good idea to call each supplier you will be sending a bid package to and request the name of an appropriate person to address the package to. Otherwise, your package may get shoved aside and neglected.

Once the bid packages have had time to arrive at the various suppliers, call and talk with your contact person. Confirm the delivery of your package and ask if there are any questions on the items you want priced. Inform the contact person not to make substitutions unless absolutely necessary, and if substitutions must be made, have the estimator note the changes in red ink. Insist that the bid be prepared in phases. For example, you might have the following phases for a kitchen job:

> Inform the contact person at your supplier not to make substitutions unless absolutely necessary, and if substitutions must be made, have the estimator note the changes in red ink.

- Framing materials
- Wall coverings
- Plumbing fixtures
- Paint
- Cabinets
- Light fixtures
- And so on

Having your bids broken down into distinct categories will make your overall evaluations easier.

GOING OVER THE QUOTES

Going over the quotes should be done when you have plenty of time and will not be disturbed. If you are in the middle of evaluating the prices and are frequently disturbed by a ringing telephone, you may overlook something of importance. The comparison process will work best if you have a large table to work at. This will allow you to lay all quotes next to each other for a quick, one-on-one comparison.

Figure 5.1 Shopping for the best material prices becomes even more essential when designing a high-end kitchen such as this. *Courtesy of Wellborn Cabinet, Inc.*

When you are reviewing quotes, do it in a quiet environment where you will not be disturbed. Avoid all distractions while you are focused on the details of quotes.

If all your quotes come back divided into the proper phases, consider yourself lucky. Suppliers don't like to go to the extra trouble to break down their bids, and they know you are more likely to spot high prices if you can compare prices side by side. Most suppliers prefer to give a lump-sum figure at the end of a computer printout. When your quotes are not broken down properly, you will have to work a little harder to determine the real meat of the bid.

What you need to do is look at the price of a 2-x-4-inch stud from each supplier. Check each supplier's price per square yard for floor covering. There is little doubt that there will be ups and downs among these items. While it makes no sense to run all over town buying studs from one supplier, nails from another, and plywood from yet another, it does make sense to shop in phases.

Not all suppliers get the same discounts on all materials. One supplier may have a great price on cabinets and a terrible price on floor coverings. It will be no great inconvenience for you to buy flooring from one store and cabinets from another.

> Savvy remodelers deal with numerous suppliers and buy their materials in phases. This allows them to maximize their profits on materials. This same strategy can work for you.

LOOKING AT THE BOTTOM LINE

Looking at the bottom line can be quite deceiving. If you look at four bids, it will be easy to see which vendor is offering the lowest overall price, but this doesn't mean it is the lowest price possible for the materials you need.

As you just learned, not all suppliers can sell the same products for the same price and make a profit even if they wanted to. There are usually some items that can be bought for less money at competitive suppliers.

By shopping the bids in phases, you will find the best prices available. You might have to deal with six different suppliers to save the most money, but you won't lose much time in doing so. There is nothing wrong in dealing with multiple suppliers.

WHAT'S INCLUDED?

What's included in each of the bids that you are comparing? Have all the suppliers include the sales tax on their bids. Generally, some suppliers will and others won't, and this can make a sizable difference in the bottom line. If the materials for your kitchen remodel cost $10,000 and the sales tax in your area is

Figure 5.2   Special amenities, such as these two sink combinations, will affect the final price of your kitchen immensely. *Photo courtesy of Moen, Inc.*

6 percent, the supplier who has included the cost of the tax will appear to be $600 higher than the suppliers who didn't include the tax. This situation is common and one you should look out for.

Will the suppliers deliver the materials for the prices quoted? This may not be a big deal if you have a truck and are only buying a few items, but if you are ordering for your whole job, delivery can be a problem and an expensive one at that. Most suppliers will deliver free of charge within a certain radius of their warehouse, but this is a question you should find the answer to before making a commitment.

Are the items you want regular in-stock items? If a supplier is quoting a job with materials that are not normally stocked, you may be faced with delays and extra hidden costs. When the supplier doesn't stock an item, you may have to pay for the shipping charges to have the item delivered to the supplier. It is unlikely that the supplier will reveal this expense in a competitive bid.

NEGOTIATING FROM PRELIMINARY PRICES

Once you have preliminary prices, you can begin the hardball negotiations. Most suppliers give professional contractors at least a 10 percent discount on the prices of materials. This discount is rarely offered to homeowners. However, if the suppliers can sell to contractors for less, they can sell to you for less. But you will have to convince them to do so.

Push suppliers for a discount after you have gotten their best price. See if you can get 10 percent off the purchase price if you pay cash for the items. This can save you substantial money.

Let's assume that you have gone over all your bids and one supplier has offered you the best prices on everything except your floor covering and plumbing fixtures. You could buy from multiple suppliers to get the best price, or you could try negotiating with the one supplier that did well on pricing the other items.

If you want to deal with just one supplier, take your other bids with you and go in for a personal visit with your sales representative. Explain how you would like to buy all of your materials from one store, but you can't justify the extra expense for the flooring and plumbing fixtures just for the sake of convenience. Ask the sales representative if anything can be done to lower the prices on the two overpriced items.

If the sales rep feels that the entire order is in jeopardy, there is a good chance that the sales manager will authorize a lower price on the flooring and plumbing fixtures. Remember, they probably have a 10 percent cushion of profit built into the entire order to work with. With a little persuasive negotiating, you can probably walk

When dealing with suppliers, don't be afraid to ask for the price you are willing to pay. If the supplier knows that you are going to the local discount supplier for homeowners rather than pay the quoted price, you might see a discount applied to your quote quickly.

away with the best price and only have to deal with one vendor.

It may also be possible to negotiate for at least a portion of the discount normally offered to contractors. A lot of contractors finance their purchases for thirty days. Since you will most likely be paying in full upon delivery, use your payment terms as leverage. Impress the sales manager with the fact that there will be no risk in collecting a bad account and that the store is not really losing any money by giving you the same discount offered to professionals.

There are plenty of ways to drive a hard bargain if you are willing to spend the time and effort to do it. Suppliers don't want to see their competition get your business, and this gives you an edge. You don't really care where the material comes from, so you can shop until you get the deal you want.

Once you have your materials secured for a good price, you may need to find and contract with some subcontractors to help you get the job done. If you will turn to the next chapter, you will see which subcontractors you might need.

6

Subcontractors

What do you know about subcontractors and their role in your project? Are you aware that the carpenter you hire to do your framing work may not have the skills or desire to do your trim work? Who hangs and sets the cabinets in the kitchen? Does a plumber install a dishwasher, or does an electrician do it? Do plumbing-and-heating companies deal with ductwork and furnaces? These questions are only a small sample of the types of questions commonly asked by homeowners.

If you are planning to act as your own general contractor, you must know what types of subcontractors will be needed for different phases of your job. Even small remodeling jobs can involve many different trades.

Once you get started on your job, you will probably become confused about the issue of subcontractors. Don't feel like you are the only one ever to be confused—many professional general contractors went through similar confusion when they got started in the business.

Today's working conditions have changed the way trades operate. It used to be that a carpenter could and would do almost any type of work that involved wood. Whether the job was making cabinets, building a barn, or hanging a door, just about any carpenter would handle the job. This is not the case today. Today's carpenters (and other tradespeople) are often highly specialized.

Since you will be searching for the best talent possible for your job, you must know what specialists to look for. Not being aware of the trends in specialization can create confusion and frustration. Imagine going through the phone book calling plumbers to help remodel your kitchen. What would your response be when you were turned down by the first five plumbers you called?

It's hard to believe a plumber would refuse to work on your remodeling job, but some will. If the plumbing company deals only in repair and service work, they will not be equipped to handle remodeling jobs. When the company does only commercial work, it will not be geared up for residential work. Plumbers who specialize in new construction will have no interest in a dirty remodeling job. To avoid this type of problem, let's take a look at each trade you may develop a need for.

TRASH CONTRACTORS

Most homeowners never think about hiring trash contractors until the rip-out debris begins to pile up. The pile of trash that accumulates during remodeling is surprising. There will be old lumber, flooring, fixtures, cardboard, and many other components of the job that must be disposed of. This is not a job that can be done reasonably using the trunk of your car. So who is going to get rid of the rubbish? This question has become harder to answer with the new rules at landfills and with the recycling efforts, but the solution is trash contractors.

SUBCONTRACTOR LIST			
Service	Vendor	Phone	Date

Figure 6.1   Example of a list for subcontractors.

Trash contractors may haul the unwanted material away in the bed of a truck or in a storage container. Most remodeling contractors rent a trash container that is placed on the job site. When the container is full, one phone call is all it takes to have it removed, emptied, and returned. There is little doubt that you will need to make some arrangements for the removal of debris.

ROUGH CARPENTERS

Rough carpenters usually do framing work. If you were building a new house, you might have a crew of rough carpenters erect the shell. In the case of remodeling, you might find one carpenter to do all the work involved, or you may have to look for different types of carpenters. If you are not expanding the size of your kitchen, you will not have much need for rough carpenters.

Some carpenters are not what they seem. It is not unusual for people to lose their jobs. When they do, some of them go out and buy a hammer so that they can call themselves carpenters. You don't want a rookie doing your remodeling. Make sure that all your contractors are experienced, licensed, and insured.

TRIM CARPENTERS

Trim carpenters are the people who hang doors, install baseboard trim and window casing, and so forth. These carpenters are good with detail work. While many of them work slowly, they often work to perfection. Some trim carpenters will install cabinets, but not all of them will. You will almost certainly need a trim carpenter.

CABINET INSTALLERS

Cabinet installers may do nothing but install cabinets. These people frequently work for companies that sell cabinets. If you were to go searching for a subcontractor to install your cabinets, you should start by asking the supplier of your cabinets for recommendations.

INSULATION CONTRACTORS

Insulation contractors are not always needed on kitchen remodeling jobs. However, if the job involves building an addition onto the home or something along those lines, an insulation contractor may be wanted. Most insulation contractors have separate crews for different types of work. If you call an insulation company, your rep should be able to organize a crew to do the work you request.

Custom cabinets can take many months to build. Getting cabinets in two months is fast for custom jobs. I talked with an employee of a custom-cabinet company a few weeks ago who told me that his company had a waiting list that was nearly a year long. Plan your cabinet delivery well in advance.

Most homeowners can install their own insulation, but many people are allergic to insulation products. If you decide to install your own insulation, protect yourself with clothing and gloves that will cover your skin. It is also wise to wear a dust mask when working with insulation.

DRYWALL HANGERS

On small jobs drywall hangers often take care of the finishing work. However, on large jobs it is not uncommon to hire one subcontractor to hang drywall and another to finish it for paint.

Drywall work is a critical part of a successful remodeling job. Make sure that your drywall contractor is reputable and check the work very closely before you pay for it.

DRYWALL FINISHERS

Drywall finishers specialize in finishing drywall. While it would be unusual to use separate contractors to hang and finish drywall on a small job, it may be to your advantage. People who spend every day finishing walls and ceilings are naturally going

SUBCONTRACTOR SCHEDULE

Type of Service	Vendor Name	Phone Number	Date Scheduled

Notes/Changes:

Figure 6.2 Example of a contractor schedule form.

SAMPLE OWNER-SUPPLIED SUBCONTRACT AGREEMENT

RICHARD & RHONDA SMART
180 HOMEOWNER LANE
WIZETOWN, OH 99897
(102) 555-6789

SUBCONTRACT AGREEMENT

This agreement, made this 25th day of July, 2004, shall set forth the whole agreement, in its entirety, between Contractor and Subcontractor.

Contractor: Richard & Rhonda Smart, referred to herein as Contractor.
Job location: 180 Homeowner Lane, Wizetown, OH
Subcontractor: Wild Bill's Painting company, referred to herein as Subcontractor.

The Contractor and Subcontractor agree to the following:

SCOPE OF WORK

Subcontractor shall perform all work as described below and provide all material to complete the work described below:

Subcontractor shall supply all labor and material to complete the work according to the attached plans and specifications. These attached plans and specifications have been initialed and signed by all parties. The work shall include, but is not limited to, the following:

(1) Scrape all painted surfaces in the family room, living room, and bedrooms.
(2) Fill all cracks and holes with joint compound.
(3) Sand painted surfaces as needed and prepare all painted surfaces for new paint.
(4) Provide protection from paint or other substance spillage.
(5) Move and replace any obstacles, furniture, or other items in the area to be painted.
(6) Prime all surfaces to be painted with an approved primer.
(7) Paint all existing painted surfaces with two coats of a Latex paint, color number LT1689.
(8) Remove any excess paint from window glass or other areas not intended to be painted.
(9) Complete all work in strict compliance with the attached plans and specifications.

(Page 1 of 3   initials _____)

Figure 6.3   Example of an owner-supplied subcontract agreement.

SAMPLE OWNER-SUPPLIED SUBCONTRACT (continued)

COMMENCEMENT AND COMPLETION SCHEDULE

The work described above shall be started within three days of verbal notice from Contractor, the projected start date is 8/20/04. The Subcontractor shall complete the above work in a professional and expedient manner by no later than twenty days from the start date. Time is of the essence in this Subcontract. No extension of time will be valid without the Contractor's written consent. If Subcontractor does not complete the work in the time allowed, and if the lack of completion is not caused by the Contractor, the Subcontractor will be charged Fifty Dollars ($50.00) per day, for every day work extends beyond the completion date. This charge will be deducted from any payments due to the Subcontractor for work performed.

CONTRACT SUM

The Contractor shall pay the Subcontractor for the performance of completed work, subject to additions and deductions, as authorized by this agreement or attached addendum. The Contract Sum is Two Thousand Dollars ($2,000.00).

PROGRESS PAYMENTS

The Contractor shall pay the Subcontractor installments as detailed below, once an acceptable insurance certificate has been filled by the Subcontractor with the Contractor:

Contractor shall pay the Subcontractor Five Hundred Dollars ($500.00), when materials are delivered and preparation work is started.

Contractor shall pay the Subcontractor Five Hundred Dollars ($500.00), when preparation work is complete and painting is started.

Contractor shall pay the Subcontractor Eight Hundred Dollars ($800.00), when all work is complete and approved by the Contractor.

Contractor shall pay the Subcontractor Two Hundred Dollars ($200.00), thirty days after completion and acceptance of work, if no deficiencies are found in materials or workmanship during the thirty day period.

All payments are subject to a site inspection and approval of work by the Contractor. Before final payment, the Subcontractor, shall submit satisfactory evidence to the Contractor that no lien risk exists on the subject property.

(Page 2 of 3 initials _____)

Figure 6.3 (*continued*)   Example of an owner-supplied subcontract agreement.

SAMPLE OWNER-SUPPLIED SUBCONTRACT (continued)

WORKING CONDITIONS

Working hours will be 8:00 a.m. through 4:30 a.m., Monday through Friday. Subcontractor is required to clean his work debris from the job site on a daily basis and leave the site in a clean and neat condition. Subcontractor shall be responsible for removal & disposal of all debris related to his job description.

CONTRACT ASSIGNMENT

Subcontractor shall not assign this contract or further subcontract the whole of this subcontract, without the written consent of the Contractor.

LAWS, PERMITS, FEES, AND NOTICES

Subcontractor shall be responsible for all required laws, permits, fees, or notices, required to perform the work stated herein.

WORK OF OTHERS

Subcontractor shall be responsible for any damage caused to existing conditions or other contractor's work. This damage will be repaired, and the Subcontractor charged for the expense and supervision of this work. The Subcontractor shall have the opportunity to quote a price for said repairs, but the Contractor is under no obligation to engage the Subcontractor to make said repairs. If a different subcontractor repairs the damage, the Subcontractor may be back-charged for the cost of the repairs.

Any repair costs will be deducted from any payments due to the Subcontractor, if any exist. If no payments are due the Subcontractor, the Subcontractor shall pay the invoiced amount within ten days.

WARRANTY

Subcontractor warrants to the Contractor, all work and materials for one year from the final day of work performed.

INDEMNIFICATION

To the fullest extent allowed by law, the Subcontractor shall indemnify and hold harmless the Owner, the Contractor, and all of their agents and employees from and against all claims, damages, losses and expenses. This agreement, entered into on July 25, 2004, shall constitute the whole agreement between Contractor and Subcontractor.

_____	_____
Contractor	Subcontractor
Richard B. Smart	Rhonda M. Smart
	(Page 3 of 3 initials _____)

Figure 6.3 (continued) Example of an owner-supplied subcontract agreement.

to be better at it than people who spend half their time hanging drywall.

WALLPAPER HANGERS

Homeowners can hang wallpaper, but wallpaper hangers specialize in this field of expertise. Using professional hangers should result in a more uniform and appealing job. If you are not experienced in working with wallpaper, it is easy to mismatch patterns and seams.

I can't begin to count the number of homeowners who have told me that they can do their own painting. It seems that nearly everyone assumes that anyone can paint. While it is true that almost anyone can apply paint to a wall or a ceiling, this does not mean that these people are real painters. Painting is more complicated than it looks. This is something that you can probably do, but don't underestimate the time and skill required for a professional painting job.

PAINTERS

Who needs painters? Anybody can paint walls and ceilings, can't they? Almost anyone can paint walls and ceilings, but professional painters tend to do a much better job than the average person would. There are many tricks of the trade when it comes to painting, and your job will benefit from the expertise of experienced painters.

ELECTRICIANS

Electricians all work with electricity, but they don't all do it in the same ways. Some electricians do only commercial work, and others do only repair work. Neither of these types of electricians will be the best choice for a remodeling job. What you need is an electrician who does residential work and preferably remodeling work. There are substantial differences between wiring a new house and wiring a remodeling job. You should spend the extra effort to find an electrician with remodeling experience.

HEATING MECHANICS

You may not have any need for heating mechanics on your job. If you are not adding space or relocating existing heating units, you won't have a need for these tradespeople. If you do have heating needs, look for mechanics who are experienced in residential remodeling. Heating mechanics are similar to electricians and plumbers in their divisions of specialization.

PLUMBERS

Plumbers specialize in all types of work. You can find plumbers who specialize in any of the following types of jobs:

- Sewer cleaning
- Well systems
- Water conditioning systems
- New construction
- Commercial work
- Residential work
- Repair work
- Remodeling
- Water-service and sewer installations

Find a plumber who knows residential remodeling inside and out.

FLOORING INSTALLERS

Flooring installers are often available through the stores that sell floor coverings. The flooring installer you hired last year to replace the carpeting in your family room may not install vinyl flooring. While most flooring installers will work with any type of carpet or vinyl, it pays to make sure you are getting someone with experience in the type of work you require.

TILE CONTRACTORS

If you want tile installed, you may need to contact tile contractors. These individuals can be found in phone directories and through the store supplying your tile.

SIDING CONTRACTORS

If you are adding space onto your home or installing new windows, you may have a need for siding contractors. Many carpenters will work with siding, but there are companies that specialize in siding work.

ROOFERS

It is unlikely that you will need roofers for an average kitchen remodel, but if you are installing skylights, bay windows, or adding space, you might. Most carpenters are willing to do minor roofing jobs, but if the work is extensive, it may be less expensive to deal directly with a roofing contractor.

Roofing work is not included in the insurance polices carried by some carpenters. If you want a carpenter to do roofing work, make sure that the contractor has the proper insurance for the job.

Now that you have a good idea of the types of subcontractors you may need, let's move on to the next chapter and see how to select the best subs for the job.

7

Selecting Contractors and Subcontractors

It is very likely that you will need at least a few subcontractors when remodeling your kitchen. Selecting your subs is a job in itself. Choosing the wrong people will turn your dream job into a nightmare. If you will be hiring a general contractor to handle the entire job for you, the burden of subcontractors will be lifted off your shoulders. However, you will still have to exercise prudence in picking a general contractor. Any way you cut it, you are going to have to deal with contractors unless you do all aspects of the job yourself.

Finding and selecting the right subcontractors are not easy tasks. I say this from experience. At one point, I was building up to sixty homes per year. That's a lot of houses and it requires a lot of help. I had some tradespeople on payroll, but subcontractors provided most of the trade labor. As I recall, I had over 120 subcontractors and vendors in any given year.

I started in the construction industry as a plumber, and my first business was a plumbing business. During that time I was a subcontractor. As my experience and business grew, I moved into remodeling and building.

CONTRACTOR SELECTION FORM

TYPE OF SERVICE	VENDOR NAME	PHONE NUMBER	DATE SCHEDULED
Site Work	N/A		
Footings	N/A		
Concrete	N/A		
Foundation	N/A		
Waterproofing	N/A		
Masonry	N/A		
Framing	J. P. Buildal	231-8294	7/3/04
Roofing	N/A		
Siding	N/A		
Exterior Trim	N/A		
Gutters	N/A		
Pest Control	N/A		
Plumbing/R-I	TMG Plumbing, Inc.	242-1987	7/9/04
HVAC/R-I	Warming's HVAC	379-9071	7/15/04
Electrical/R-I	Bright Electric	257-2225	7/18/04
Central Vacuum	N/A		
Insulation	Allstar Insulators	242-4792	7/24/04
Drywall	Hank's Drywall	379-6638	7/29/04
Painter	J. C. Brush	247-8931	8/15/04
Wallpaper	N/A		
Tile	N/A		
Cabinets	N/A		
Countertops	N/A		
Interior Trim	The Final Touch Co.	365-1962	8/8/04
Floor Covering	Carpet Magicians	483-8724	8/19/04
Plumbing/Final	Same	Same	8/21/04
HVAC/Final	Same	Same	8/22/04
Electrical/Final	Same	Same	8/23/04
Cleaning	N/A		
Paving	N/A		
Landscaping	N/A		

NOTES/CHANGES _____

Figure 7.1 Example of a contractor selection form.

It was then that I became a general contractor. Having been a subcontractor and having worked around other subcontractors, I had more experience on the subject of subcontractors than most new general contractors. Even so, finding, choosing, and keeping the best subs was a chore, and it still is.

I have given you this brief background to prove two points. I have extensive experience in working with subcontractors. And if a professional has to continue to work at finding and selecting good subs, a homeowner should not take the task lightly.

WHERE SHOULD YOU LOOK FOR SUBCONTRACTORS?

Where should you look for subcontractors? The advertising pages of your local phone book are a logical place to start. Contractors listed in the phone book have been established in business for at least a little while, and they are easy to locate.

Newspapers

Local newspapers are another good place to look for subcontractors. The rates for advertising in phone books are steep, and some good contractors have nothing more than a line listing in the

> Don't assume that all contractors who have ads in the phone book are reputable. It only takes money to buy ads. The skills that your job will require include much more than money. But a contractor who is listed in the phone book is a good place to start.

phone directory. These contractors prefer to spend their advertising budget selectively, and the newspaper is one of the places they may use to announce their services to the public.

Friends

Ask your friends if they know of any reputable contractors. It is hard to beat trusted word-of-mouth referrals when searching for good contractors.

Look for Signs

When you are riding around your neighborhood, look for signs that indicate the presence of remodelers working in your area.

When checking the references of contractors, ask to be shown some of the jobs that they have completed, but also ask to see jobs in progress. The jobs in progress will be easier to gain access to, and it will give you a better view of the work as it is being done at the present time. This is an advantage.

Many contractors display signs with their company names and phone numbers when doing a job. Finding contractors this way shows you that they are working, and you can probably gain permission to inspect the work they are involved with for others.

WHAT QUALITIES SHOULD YOU LOOK FOR IN SUBCONTRACTORS?

What qualities should you look for in subcontractors? In some cases the qualities will vary with the different types of contractors, but there are some common attributes to seek.

Licensing

Any contractor you hire should be licensed to conduct business. Many trades, such as plumbing, heating, and electrical contracting require special licensing. For example, a plumbing contractor should hold a master plumber's license. Having a journeyman plumbing license is not sufficient for most plumbing contracting.

Check with your local code and licensing authorities to determine which licenses are required for various types of work, and don't associate yourself with contractors who are not properly licensed.

Insurance

Check to see that any contractors being considered for your job are properly insured. Insurance for contractors is expensive, and many contractors don't have insurance. Hiring an uninsured contractor is very risky business.

Experience

Experience in remodeling is vital to the successful completion of your job. It is easy for contractors to say they have years of experience with remodeling work. Make them prove it! Contractors who work with new construction are not always qualified remodelers. The differences between remodeling and new work are significant.

References

Since you will be requiring contractors to prove their experience in remodeling, check the references they provide you with. Insist on at least five references. Shady contractors will be expecting you to ask for three references, and they may have three friends or relatives prepared to pose as references. By asking for five references you may be able to catch crooked contractors off guard. Ideally, you should visit jobs the contractors are doing to see that the references you are given are real.

When you verify a contractor's insurance, verify it with the agency issuing the insurance policy. Don't take the contractor's word for it. If you are reviewing a certificate of insurance on a contractor, examine the dates carefully because the policy may have expired.

You can hire a very experienced contractor and still have the wrong contractor for your job. Make sure that the contractor's experience is in the field related to your type of work. In short, don't hire a commercial heating company to relocate your residential ductwork. The commercial crew may be able to do the job without hesitation, but you should be better off with a company experienced in residential remodeling.

Business Stability

Business stability in remodeling and contracting can be difficult to maintain. Swings in the economy can turn a company that was thriving the year before into a bankrupt business. Some businesses that present a strong public image can be on the verge of collapse. You trust your money and your house to these contractors, and you are entitled to know that your trust is not misplaced.

PHONE LOG			
Date	Company Name	Contact Person	Remarks

Figure 7.2 Example of a phone log.

HOW CAN YOU VERIFY INFORMATION GIVEN TO YOU BY SUBS?

How can you verify information given to you by subs? Insurance information can be verified by calling the insurance agency providing coverage to the subcontractor. References can be called, but whenever possible they should be visited. Licensing information can be verified with the licensing agencies in your area. Experience is difficult to verify, but checking references will provide some security.

If the contractor will give permission for you to talk with material suppliers, the suppliers can tell you much about the stability of the contractor's business. Requesting permission to talk with the contractor's bank is another way to check for business stability.

> Dig deep and find out as much as you can about the contractors and the stability of their businesses.

Many contractors belong to professional organizations that may be willing to provide some background information. Credit reports on the contractors would be of help, but few contractors are going to provide homeowners with the same verifications they will offer a professional general contractor.

Getting answers to all your questions will not be easy. Many subcontractors will consider your requests unusual and more trouble than your business is worth. Since most homeowners ask very few questions of contractors, the few that do face an uphill battle. While you can't expect to be completely safe working with subs, you can hedge the odds by learning as much about the contractors as possible.

CHOOSE BACKUP SUBCONTRACTORS RIGHT FROM THE START.

When you begin selecting subs, choose backup subcontractors right from the start. Invariably, there are times when the subcontractors you want to do the job will not work out. Sometimes they will be injured and unable to perform the work. There will be occasions when the contractors are behind schedule and cannot get to your job when they are supposed

Wise professionals always have at least three subcontractors for every phase of work. Having three electricians chosen in advance will allow more freedom and less chance for a catastrophe than putting all your trust in one subcontractor.

If you are told you should remodel your bathroom at the same time that you are having your kitchen remodeled, think the proposition over. There is a good chance that you could save money by having both jobs done simultaneously, but if your bathroom doesn't need to be remodeled, you are wasting your money.

to. Some contractors will seem to just disappear, and you won't be able to find them to do the work. It is better that this happens before work is started than after. There are dozens of reasons for selecting backup contractors.

When you are sorting through potential contractors, give them ratings. For example, when considering drywall contractors, establish a first, second, and third choice for your job. This type of advance planning may save you much trouble once the job is started.

BEWARE OF SALES HYPE

Beware of sales hype. Some contractors are better at selling their services than providing them. As a consumer, you must screen all contractors carefully and avoid camouflaged salespeople. The best salespeople will not appear to be selling you anything. True professionals can make you buy products and services you don't need and don't want. Learning this from experience can be very costly.

You can protect yourself from impulse buying by refusing to make an on-the-spot decision. When you are told that if you don't act immediately the price will go up, look for another contractor.

SATISFACTION

To achieve satisfaction from your completed job, you may need dependable, reputable, experienced subcontractors. Spend enough time in the selection process to ensure your satisfaction. The wrong contractors can turn the best job into a horror show, but the right contractors can make difficult work look easy.

The Masters Group, Inc.

PMB # 300 13 Gurnet Road
Brunswick, Maine 04011
207-729-8357 (Phone)
207-798-5070 (Fax)
tmg1@mfx.net (Email)

SUBCONTRACTOR AGREEMENT

This agreement, made this _____ day of _____, 20__, shall set forth the whole agreement, in its entirety, between The Masters Group, Inc., hereafter referred to as Contractor, and Subcontractor.

Job location: _____

Subcontractor: _____, referred to herein as Subcontractor.

The Contractor and Subcontractor agree to the following.

ORIGINAL CONTRACT

Contractor has entered into a contract, hereinafter referred to as the original contract, dated _____, with the owner wihich includes the work to be performed under and pursuant to this subcontract agreement.

SCOPE OF WORK

Subcontractor shall perform all work as described below and provide all material to complete the work described below.

Subcontractor shall supply all labor and material to complete the work according to the original contract with the owner and the attached plans and specifications. These attached plans and specifications have been initialed and signed by all parties. The work shall include, but is not limited to, the following: _____

_____
_____
_____
_____
_____
_____
_____
_____

(Page 1 of 4. Please initial _____.)

Figure 7.3   Subcontractor agreement

COMMENCEMENT AND COMPLETION SCHEDULE

The work described above shall be started within _____ (____) days of verbal notice from Contractor, the projected start date is _____. The Subcontractor shall complete the above work in a professional and expedient manner by no later than _____ (____) days from the start date. Time is of the essence in this contract. No extension of time will be valid without the Contractor's written consent. If Subcontractor does not complete the work in the time allowed, and if the lack of completion is not caused by the Contractor, the Subcontractor will be charged _____ ($_____) dollars per day, for every day work extends beyond the completion date. This charge will be deducted from any payments due to the Subcontractor for work performed.

CONTRACT SUM

The Contractor shall pay the Subcontractor for the performance of completed work subject to additions and deductions as authorized by this agreement or attached addendum. The contract sum is _____($_____).

DUE DATE FOR RECEIPT OF PAYMENTS FROM OWNER

The due date for receipt of payment from the owner is _____.

PROGRESS PAYMENTS

The Contractor shall pay the Subcontractor installments as detailed below, once an acceptable insurance certificate has been filed by the Subcontractor with the Contractor. Contractor shall pay the Subcontractor as described: _____
_____
_____

The Subcontractor shall be paid upon 7 days after receipt of each progress or final payment by the owner or 7 days after receipt of the subcontractor's or material supplier's invoice, whichever is later. Payments are subject to retainage for uncompleted performance. Retainage shall be paid prior to thirty days after final acceptance of the work. All payments are subject to a site inspection and approval of work by the Contractor. Before final payment, the Subcontractor shall submit satisfactory evidence to the Contractor that no lien risk exists on the subject property and Subcontractor shall supply an executed lien waiver.

WORKING CONDITIONS

Working hours will be _____ a.m. through _____ p.m., Monday through Friday. Subcontractor is required to clean work debris from the job site on a daily basis and leave the site in a clean and neat condition. Subcontractor shall be responsible for removal and disposal of all debris related to the job description.

REIMBURSEMENT FOR DAMAGES OF COST

Subcontractor shall reimburse contractor for any actual damages or costs incurred by reason of subcontractor's failure to prosecute the work diligently, including any liquidated damages assessed by owner pursuant to the original contract.

(Page 2 of 4. Please initial _____.)

Figure 7.3 (continued)　Subcontractor agreement

TAKEOVER BY CONTRACTOR

Should subcontractor fail or neglect to proceed diligently, timely, competently, or in a competent manner, or should subcontractor by delaying, interfering with, or jeopardizing the timely or satisfactory completion of the work under the original contract, then and in that event contractor, in its sole discretion, reserves the right, after giving 48 hours notice, written or oral, to take over the work and complete such work at the cost and expense of subcontractor, without prejudice to contractor's other rights or remedies for any loss or damages sustained, and in the event of such takeover, subcontractor agrees that no material, machine, or tools belonging to subcontractor shall be removed from the job until completion. Previous demands made on subcontractor not followed by a takeover shall not be deemed a waiver of contractor's rights to do so.

CONTRACT ASSIGNMENT

Subcontractor shall not assign this contract or further subcontract the whole of this subcontract, without the written consent of the Contractor.

LAWS, PERMITS, FEES, AND NOTICES

Subcontractor shall be responsible for all required laws, permits, fees, or notices, required to perform the work stated herein.

WORK OF OTHERS

Subcontractor shall be responsible for any damage caused to existing conditions or other contractor's work. This damage will be repaired, and the Subcontractor charged for the expense and supervision of this work. The Subcontractor shall have the opportunity to quote a price for said repairs, but the Contractor is under no obligation to engage the Subcontractor to make said repairs. If a different subcontractor repairs the damage, the Subcontractor may be backcharged for the cost of the repairs. Any repair costs will be deducted from any payments due to the Subcontractor. If no payments are due the Subcontractor, the Subcontractor shall pay the invoiced amount within _____ (_____) days.

WARRANTY

Subcontractor warrants and guarantees the work and materials covered by this subcontract and agrees to make good, at its own expense, any defect in materials or work thay may occur or develop prior to contractor's release from responsibility to owner for such materials or work.

(Page 3 of 4. Please initial _____.)

Figure 7.3 (*continued*)   Subcontractor agreement

INDEMNIFICATION

To the fullest extent allowed by law, the Subcontractor shall assume full responsibility for its employees, officers, agents, and business invitees. Subcontractor hereby agrees to indemnify and hold and save Contractor harmless from and against any claim, demand, action or cause of action that may be asserted by any person arising out of any damage, loss, expense, injury or death suffered by any of subcontractor's employees, officers, agents, and business invitees and regardless of the sole or concurring negligence of the contractor. Subcontractor shall indemnify contractor and owner against any and all loss, damages, cost, expenses, and attorney fees suffered or incurred on account of any breach of the obligations and covenants any any other provision or covenant of this subcontract

LEGAL ACTION

Should legal action be required, this agreement shall be interpreted under the laws of the State of Maine. Any dispute, controversy, or claim arising out of or relating to this agreement, or the breach of this agreement, shall be subject to the jurisdiction of the courts of Cumberland County, in the State of Maine. The parties hereby designate the venue of Cumberland County, in the State of Maine, as the forum for the resolution of all disputes, controversies, or claims arising out of or relating to this agreement, or the breach of this agreement. The Subcontractor consents to and acknowledges personal jurisdiction over the Subcontractor by such Court and the Subcontractor agrees to be subject to the personal jurisdiction of the State of Maine.

If there is any portion of this agreement that the Subcontractor does not understand fully, the Subcontractor is encouraged to seek competent legal counsel prior to executing this contractual agreement.

This agreement, entered into on _____, 20____, shall constitute the whole agreement between Contractor and Subcontractor.

Contractor	Date	Subcontractor	Date
The Masters Group, Inc.			

Figure 7.3 (continued)   Subcontractor agreement

8

Dealing with Contractors

H ow well you deal with contractors can have a strong influence on the cost of your job. The prices contractors quote for similar work can span a broad spectrum. The same could be said for any subcontractors you might need. Even if the difference in hourly rates is only $10, the cost over the course of the job can amount to quite a bit.

Let's look at a quick example of how the hourly rates used by two plumbers in estimating a kitchen-remodeling job might affect your costs. One plumber is pricing labor at $52 an hour, and the other is figuring $62 an hour. Both plumbers are figuring the same amount of time for the work required.

When the plumbers estimate the time they will devote to removing existing fixtures, they figure five hours plus travel and miscellaneous time. To round it off, they both consider the rip-out to be worth eight hours of their time.

When figuring the labor for setting new fixtures, both plumbers arrive at an estimate of another eight hours. Allowing for inspections, handling material acquisitions, and other administrative duties will be billed as an additional eight hours.

Using broad-brush estimating techniques, both plumbers have arrived at estimates of 24 hours for their involvement in your remodeling job. The highest estimate is $1,488 and the lowest estimate is $1,248. There is about a 17 percent difference in the costs, and this is just for the plumbing phase of the job.

Assume that the total cost for all labor in your kitchen-remodeling job will cost $6,000. If you could shave 17 percent off that labor figure, you would save $1,020. Is it possible to save this much money and still get a good job? Yes, it is possible, but it will require effort on your part.

Finding the best deals on labor takes patience and persistence. Contractors are not going to give their services away, but they may be willing to discount them heavily if you know the right buttons to push. There are ways to convince contractors to give you a lower price for the privilege of getting your job. Why would contractors do this for you? That's what you are about to find out.

Think twice before you agree to let a contractor use your job as fill-in work. This is rarely a good idea for kitchen remodeling. Why? You could be without your facilities for much longer than you wish to be.

FILL-IN WORK

All contractors love to have fill-in work. This is work they can do when circumstances prohibit them from doing regularly scheduled work. If it is a rainy day and a carpenter cannot work outside, having a fill-in job that allows inside work is a welcome pleasure. If a delivery is mixed up on one job and brings a crew to a halt, the contractor will not lose as much money if the crew can be sent to work on a fill-in job.

Due to the nature of fill-in jobs, they don't get finished quickly. If you are willing to allow your work to drag out for weeks or perhaps months, you are in a good position to bargain for a lower price. However, if you need the work completely in a timely fashion, don't consider a fill-in job.

The Masters Group, Inc.

PMB # 300 13 Gurnet Road
Brunswick, Maine 04011
207-729-8357 (Phone)
207-798-5070 (Fax)
tmg1@mfx.net (Email)

PROPOSAL

Date: _____

Customer name: _____

Address: _____

Phone number: _____

Job location: _____

DESCRIPTION OF WORK

The Masters Group, Inc. will supply, and or coordinate, all labor and material for the above referenced job as follows: _____

_____

_____

_____

The following work is the responsibility of the owner or contractors hired by the owner:

_____

_____

WORK SCHEDULE

The Masters Group, Inc. will commence work on, or about, _____.
Work is anticipated to be completed, subject to weather, the work of others, and the availability of materials, by _____.

(Page 1 of 4. Please initial _____.)

Figure 8.1 Proposal

PAYMENT SCHEDULE

Price: _____ dollars ($_____)
or, the price will be based upon a time-and material basis at a labor rate of _____
and the price of materials as stated by The Masters Group, Inc. A deposit will be paid in the
amount of _____ (not to exceed 1/3 of the total price) with additional payments to
be made as follows: _____
_____

All payments shall be made in full, upon presentation of each completed invoice. If payment is
not made according to the terms above, The Masters Group, Inc. may cease work on the project
until all invoices are paid and may lien the property where the work has been done in
accordance with Maine law. The Masters Group, Inc. may use all legal methods in the
collection of monies owed to it.

Should legal action be required, this agreement shall be interpreted under the laws of the State
of Maine. Any dispute, controversy, or claim arising out of or relating to this agreement, or the
breach of this agreement, shall be subject to the jurisdiction of the courts of Cumberland
County, in the State of Maine. The parties hereby designate the venue of Cumberland County,
in the State of Maine, as the forum for the resolution of all disputes, controversies, or claims
arising out of or relating to this agreement, or the breach of this agreement. The Customer
consents to and acknowledges personal jurisdiction over the Customer by such Court and the
Customer agrees to be subject to the personal jurisdiction of the State of Maine.

WARRANTIES

The contractor provides the following express warranty:
_____
_____
_____

In addition to any additional express warranties agreed to by the parties, the contractor warrants
that the work will be free from faulty materials; constructed according to the standards of the
building code applicable for this location; constructed in a skillful manner and fit for habitation.
The warranty rights and remedies set forth in the Maine Uniform Commercial Code apply to
this contract.

(Page 2 of 4. Please initial _____.)

Figure 8.1 (continued)   Proposal

RESOLUTION OF DISPUTES

If a dispute arises concerning the provisions of this contract or the performance by the parties, then the parties agree to settle this dispute by jointly paying for one of the following (check only one):
(1) Binding arbitration as regulated by the Maine Uniform Arbitration Act, with the parties agreeing to accept as final the arbitrator's decision (_____);
(2) Nonbinding arbitration, with the parties free to not accept the arbitrator's decision and to seek satisfaction through other means, including a lawsuit (_____);
(3) Mediation, with the parties agreeing to enter into good faith negotiations through a neutral mediator in order to attempt to resolve their differences (_____);
The parties are *not* required to select one of these dispute resolution methods. They are optional. If the parties do *not* select one of these dispute resolution options, check here: _____.

CHANGE ORDERS

Any alteration or deviation from the above contractual specifications that involve extra cost will be executed *only upon the parties entering into a written change order*.

If this contract includes construction of a new residential building or a new addition to an existing residence, it must contain a statement that 10 M.R.S.A. §§ 1411 - 1420 establishes minimum energy efficient building standards for new residential construction, and whether this building or addition will meet or exceed those standards.

If there is any portion of this agreement that the Customer does not understand fully, the Customer is encouraged to seek competent legal counsel prior to executing this contractual agreement.

If the job is not ready for the service or materials requested, as scheduled, and the delay is not due to the actions of The Masters Group, Inc., The Masters Group, Inc. may charge the Customer for lost time. This charge will be at a rate of $_____ per hour, per worker, including travel time.

If you have any questions or don't understand this proposal, seek professional advice. Upon acceptance, this proposal becomes a binding contract between both parties.

Respectfully submitted,

Roger Woodson, President

(Page 3 of 4. Please initial _____.)

Figure 8.1 (*continued*)   Proposal

ACCEPTANCE

We the undersigned do hereby agree to, and accept, all the terms and conditions of this proposal. We fully understand the terms and conditions, and hereby consent to enter into this contract.

The Masters Group, Inc.   Customer

By: _____   _____

Title: _____   Date: _____

Date: _____

Proposal expires in 30 days, if not accepted by all parties.

Figure 8.1 (*continued*)   Proposal

Since fill-in jobs are valuable to contractors, you can often negotiate for a lower price if you are willing to allow your work to be a fill-in job. This works well with some types of home improvements, but it usually is not a good idea with kitchen remodeling

REFERENCE JOBS

Reference jobs are not always easy for contractors to come by. What is a reference job? A reference job is a job that a contractor can give as a reference to future customers. If appointments can be scheduled with the homeowners of completed jobs for showing the work to prospective customers, contractors can close more sales. Any progressive contractor recognizes the value of having jobs that can be shown to potential customers.

If you structure a deal with contractors to use your house as an example of their work, you win two ways. First, you win by getting a lower price for the services you receive. Secondly, you win because since the job will be used to show off the contractors' talents, you will get the benefit of the best job the contractors can do.

Allowing your job to be used as a showplace is a very effective way to negotiate for better pricing and sometimes for better materials. Remember, the contractors will be showing the job to future customers, and the business owners will want their new customers to be favorably impressed. However, if you do agree to such an arrangement, establish the terms in writing. Dictate how much notice you will be given prior to showings, how long your job will be used as a reference, and how many showings will be allowed on a weekly basis.

> Just as you should arrange to see samples of a contractor's work, so should other customers. If you are willing to allow contractors to use your job as a reference job, you should receive something for the inconvenience of being a good reference for the contractor. This something can often be a lower price for the work being done.

NEW COMPANIES

New companies are frequently starved for work and references. Dealing with the right new companies can save you considerable money. If you happen to deal with the wrong new companies, the pain will out-weigh the advantages. Choose your contractors carefully.

New companies are frequently starved for work and references. Dealing with the right new companies can save you considerable money. If you happen to deal with the wrong new companies, the pain will outweigh the advantages. Choose your contractors carefully.

When contractors first go into business for themselves, they need work badly. Many of these new business owners are not new to their business, only to owning it. The contractors could have twenty years of experience doing their job but have only been in business for a month.

There are risks to dealing with fledgling companies, but there are also rewards. If the contractors are honest and experienced, you can get better service than you might from a large, established company, and the price will almost always be less.

Should you decide to gamble on using a new company? Do your homework. Make sure that the business is insured and licensed. While there may not be much to investigate, dig up everything you can on the company and its owner.

NEGOTIATE

Don't be afraid to negotiate with contractors. When you go to buy a new car, do you automatically agree to pay the full price on the window sticker? If you haggle over the price of a car, why shouldn't you negotiate for a better price from contractors? In many cases the full price of a major remodeling job is more than the cost of an average new car, so certainly there is enough money involved to be worth negotiating. Many homeowners never question the prices given by contractors. They either look elsewhere for a lower price or accept the price they are given.

I have been involved in construction for about thirty years. Many of these years have been as a contractor, and I have rarely had homeowners dicker with me on prices. As a subcontractor I have had plenty of general contractors bargain for better prices, but few homeowners ever do. This is a situation I have never really understood.

Very few contractors show all their cards on the initial bid, They bid jobs expecting to negotiate. When homeowners accept the bid as is, the contractors pocket some extra profits. If homeowners look at the prices and continue to search for other, lower-priced contractors, the contractors with the padded bids lose out.

If you have found a contractor who fits the perfect profile, don't let a high bid alienate you. Good contractors are hard to find, and when you do find one, you should make an effort to work out a viable deal. Contractors are not so different from other business owners that they are unwilling to consider offers and negotiations.

While many good contractors don't inflate their prices enormously, most do build in a buffer of at least 5 percent. It is not unusual for contractors to inflate their prices by 10 percent. Knowing this, you should try to squeeze that price cushion out of the contractors. Saving 5 percent on a $20,000 kitchen job means saving $1,000. While $1,000 is not enough to retire on, it is enough to pay for a new microwave and dishwasher.

REMODEL WITH THE SEASONS

When you remodel with the seasons of the year, you can save money. There are certain times of the year when contractors traditionally have less work than they would like. If you can arrange to have your job done during the off-season, many contractors will reward you with a lower price.

What is the best time of the year to have your remodeling done? There are several good times of the year for you to take advantage of special prices and incentives. Let's start with the first of the year and look at each month to establish your best buying times.

Following are the months of the year and the pros and cons of each for getting your best deal:

CONTRACTOR RATING SHEET

Job name: _____   Date: _____

Category	Contractor 1	Contractor 2	Contractor 3
Contractor name			
Returns calls			
Licensed			
Insured			
Bonded			
References			
Price			
Experience			
Years in business			
Work quality			
Availability			
Deposit required			
Detailed quote			
Personality			
Punctual			
Gut reaction			

Notes: _____

_____

_____

_____

_____

_____

_____

Figure 8.2   Example of a contractor rating form.

- January: January is an excellent time to schedule your remodeling work. Many homeowners are still recovering from the holiday season and adjusting to the new tax year. In most regions the weather during January is not conducive to construction and happy attitudes. This makes the first month of the year a good time to save some money on your remodeling costs.

- February: February is often cold and dreary—an excellent time to offer contractors inside work. However, February is also the month when many contractors are getting geared up for the spring rush, so they may not be quite as flexible as they would be in January.

- March: March is a month when the odds favor contractors. People who have been depressed through the winter see a glimmer of hope for warm, sunny days, and they are more likely to have a positive outlook. This change in attitude often results in buying things: home improvements, houses, cars, and so on. Avoid the month of March.

- April: April is another month to avoid. By April, people are sure summer is getting closer, and they are ready to go on spending sprees. This is not a good time to look for bargains in home improvements.

- May: May does not offer any better opportunities than April. The spring months are the worst choices for home-improvement values.

- June: June is not appreciably better than April or May. It is another month to avoid.

- July: July can offer some windows of opportunity for bargain shoppers. Many people vacation in July, and this results in less work for contractors. The heat of July can also make contractors look for inside work, where air conditioning will temper the heat. While July is not the hottest month for home-improvement values, it is better than the months of spring.

- August: August is a good time to have inside work done. Oppressive heat in many parts of the country makes contractors dream of working in air-conditioned spaces. Another advantage to August is that many parents are getting their children ready to go back to school or college. The preoccupation with the costs and duties of getting the kids back in school prevents these people from pursuing remodeling work. Their lack of interest in remodeling during August will work to your advantage.

- September: September is no good for discount remodeling prices. This is a month when many people decide to remodel before winter, so avoid shopping in September.

- October: October is worse than September for bargain hunting. People are rushing about to get their homes in order before the holidays, and contractors have no shortage of work during these times.

- November: By the middle of November, the remodeling market becomes a buyer's market. Most people don't want contractors in their homes during Thanksgiving, and this opens the door of opportunity to lower prices for you.

- December: December is an excellent month for low remodeling prices. Most people don't contemplate remodeling between Thanksgiving and Christmas. This gives you ample opportunity to cash in with some hefty savings. It also doesn't hurt that contractors often want extra money for Christmas.

A creative homeowner can find numerous levers to manipulate contractors into lower prices. If you put your mind to it, you should be able to save substantial money on your job by strategic shopping and negotiating.

9

Code Considerations

Permits and code compliance are considerations that all homeowners involved with remodeling projects should be aware of. If you will be doing your own remodeling work, these aspects of the job are of the utmost importance. When you hire a general contractor to do the job for you, you shouldn't have to worry about code compliance and permits, but if you are smart, you will take the time to learn at least in general terms what should and shouldn't be done.

Unfortunately, not all contractors play by the rules. Some contractors avoid getting permits for their jobs to keep the price of the work lower. A few contractors are unable to get permits because they are not licensed and therefore never inform their customers of a need for permits and inspections. For whatever the reason, it is not a good idea to perform work that requires a permit and inspection without the proper authorization.

Any work done that does not comply with code requirements may have to be torn out and done over again. If you were unlucky enough to hook up with a bad contractor, you might wind up paying for the contractor's mistakes, and this can get expensive very quickly.

Require all contractors who are responsible for the acquisition of permits and inspections to furnish you with copies of the inspection approvals. Don't pay completion fees to contractors without proof that their work has been inspected and approved, as required by your local code-enforcement office.

Almost every town, city, and county has a code-enforcement office and official code inspectors. The inspectors are employed to protect the citizens of the jurisdiction, including you. While arranging for code inspections may not be something you want to do, it may be required by law in your area, and the inspection may protect you from all sorts of dangers.

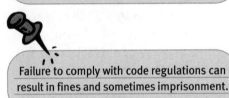

If you will be doing work that requires a permit yourself, you can apply for one as a homeowner. Owners who reside in their property can be issued permits that would normally require professional licensing.

DOES ALL WORK HAVE TO BE INSPECTED?

Does all work have to be inspected? No, not all work requires a permit or an inspection, but much of the work involved with kitchen remodeling does require permits and inspections.

Failure to comply with code regulations can result in fines and sometimes imprisonment.

When permits are required, they must be obtained before any work regulated under the permit is started. The permits are normally required to be posted on the job in a conspicuous place where they can be seen from the street.

WHAT'S INVOLVED IN GETTING A PERMIT?

What's involved with getting a permit? Getting a permit is not difficult, but there are guidelines that must be followed. The procedure for obtaining a permit can vary from jurisdiction to

Figure 9.1 Working carefully to comply with code requirements can make this exquisite kitchen a reality. *Courtesy of Wellborn Cabinet, Inc.*

jurisdiction. Check with your local code authorities for exact details on what the requirements are in your area.

Typically, a set of plans and specifications must be submitted to the code-enforcement office, along with a completed permit application (available from the code office) to receive a permit. Payment for the permit is also required.

Some types of work may not require plans and specifications to be submitted. Under these conditions, the only paperwork involved will be the permit application. There will be a fee for the permit if it is issued. The amounts of fees vary from location to location, but the costs for all the permits needed for a major remodeling job can run into hundreds of dollars. Most single permits will be less than $75, and many will be less than $50.

If you apply for your own permits, be advised that normally permits are only issued to homeowners who will be performing the work themselves and to licensed contractors. If

Do not obtain permits in your name and then allow unlicensed people to do the work for you. This could land you in significant trouble. If you are thinking of skirting the issue of an unlicensed contractor by getting the permit yourself, forget it. The risk is not worth it.

you apply for the permit in your name and hire an unlicensed person to do the work for you, there could be trouble if you are caught.

Once the permit has been applied for, a code officer will review the application. If all the paperwork is in order, the permit fee will be paid (by you or your contractor) and the permit will be issued. The permit should be posted at your home in such a way that an inspector can see it from the street.

WHAT TYPES OF WORK REQUIRE PERMITS?

What types of work require permits? Most small jobs that are mostly repairs or maintenance don't normally require permits and inspections, but larger jobs do. Let's look at where permits are likely to be needed for your job:

- Plumbing: Plumbing work almost always requires a permit and inspection. Unless all you are doing is very minor remodeling or repair work, plan on getting a plumbing permit. Normally, if you are relocating fixtures, adding fixtures, or doing extensive work with plumbing pipes, a permit and inspections will be required.

- Electrical: Electrical work is similar to plumbing in terms of permits and inspections. If you are adding a circuit, relocating wiring, or work of this nature, a permit will probably be required.

- HVAC: Heating and air-conditioning work is also normally done with the use of a permit. Very minor changes will not require a permit or inspection, but if you are expanding your HVAC system or making significant changes in outlet locations, you may need a permit.

- Building: Building permits are normally required whenever a new structure is built, but they may not be required for cosmetic remodeling. However, if you will be making structural changes to your home, a permit is likely to be required.

To be safe, you should inquire at your local code-enforcement office for information on what is required of you. Code requirements can change quickly, and every jurisdiction can have its own set of rules.

KEEP YOUR CONTRACTORS HONEST

Keep your contractors honest. If a permit and inspection are required for the work being done, insist that the contractors comply with the regulations. While it may not be your responsibility to see that contractors obtain the proper permits, you may be the one to suffer in the end. Make it your responsibility to supervise the acquisition of permits and the completion of required inspections.

How could a contractor's violation of code requirements hurt you? Serious violations could jeopardize your health and safety. For example, there are many plumbing-code requirements that exist for your protection. If an air gap is not installed with the drainage system of a dishwasher, it is possible that contaminated water in the drainage pipes will flow back into the dishwasher, creating a health hazard. If a plumber omits a required vent pipe, you may suffer from the effects of sewer gas. Water heaters that are installed without relief valves can blow up, causing death and destruction.

An electrician's failure to install a ground-fault interceptor could result in a fatal shock. Aside from the more deadly infractions, minor code violations can make your job less functional. If electrical outlets are not installed at the prescribed minimum distances, you may have an appliance with an electrical cord that is too short to reach an outlet.

Figure 9.2 Imagine the heartbreak and expense if this beautiful kitchen had to be torn apart due to code violations. *Courtesy of Wellborn Cabinet, Inc.*

If a heating technician installs heating units in the wrong locations, the performance of the heating system may not be satisfactory. All these possible code violations can present you with unwanted circumstances.

In addition to the health risks and inconveniences you might encounter with work done in a non-conforming manner, you might lose a substantial amount of money because of the violations. Suppose an electrician gave you a great price for rewiring your kitchen and did the job without a permit. What might happen? Here are some possibilities:

- The house could burn down.

- You could be electrocuted.

- An electrical inspector from the code enforcement-office might require all the kitchen walls to be torn open so the wiring could be inspected when the illegal job was discovered. That's right! The inspector could insist that you rip out your newly remodeled walls to expose all wiring that should have been inspected prior to concealment.

If you are forced to destroy your new job for the sake of an inspection that was never done, who is going to pay for the damage? It seems that the offending contractor should, but suppose the contractor has gone out of business or left town. You may be left holding the responsibility. Don't set yourself up for this type of disaster. Make sure all your work is done in compliance with code requirements.

10

Financing Your Project

What is involved in financing your remodeling effort? Can you just walk into your bank and ask for a loan and get it? Should you take out a personal loan to pay for the job, or should you refinance your house to cover the costs? These are only some of the questions that may come up before you begin work on your remodeling project.

Major remodeling jobs often cost more than $10,000, and this forces a lot of people to seek financing. Since the average person is not accustomed to working with financing, the task of finding and selecting the best loan can be an arduous one. Just as there are many types of products and designs to choose from for your job, there are also many forms of financing to consider.

DOES THE TYPE OF FINANCING YOU CHOOSE REALLY MAKE A DIFFERENCE?

Does the type of financing you choose really make a difference? It can make a big difference in the long-term cost of your job. The interest you pay on the loan will increase the overall cost of your remodeling work. If you have to pay a lender financing points to originate the loan, you will need more money to start the job, and the amortized interest will increase the long-term cost of the job.

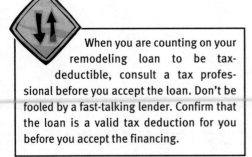

When you are counting on your remodeling loan to be tax-deductible, consult a tax professional before you accept the loan. Don't be fooled by a fast-talking lender. Confirm that the loan is a valid tax deduction for you before you accept the financing.

Your choice in loans can also affect how much you pay in income taxes. If you arrange the loan as a part of your home mortgage, the interest on the loan may be deductible. When the interest payments are deductible and result in fewer taxes to be paid, the job does not cost as much as it would with a loan where the interest was not tax-deductible.

If you are thinking of selling your home, the financing you choose could hamper the sale. Assume that your house has an assumable mortgage with an attractive interest rate. Selling the house with the assumable loan may give you a great advantage in a real-estate market with high interest rates. However, if you refinance the house at current interest rates to pay for a new kitchen, you have lost your edge in the sales market.

The selection of financing is a responsibility that should not be taken lightly. Not only is selecting the right financing important, but knowing how to apply for it can make a big difference in whether your loan is approved. Let's take a close look at how financing will play a role in your remodeling plans.

FIXED-RATE LOANS

Fixed-rate loans are the loans most people are best informed about. These loans operate on a simple principle: you borrow money at an agreed-upon interest rate and the rate never changes. The biggest advantage to this type of loan is that you know what your payments will be for every installment over the life of the loan. The biggest disadvantage to a fixed-rate

Figure 10.1 A more luxurious kitchen may be possible with the help of creative financing. *Courtesy of Wellborn Cabinet, Inc.*

loan is that, because the interest rate is fixed, it is usually higher when the loan is obtained than rates for other types of loans are.

If you plan to keep your house for at least the next ten years and you are not much of a gambler, fixed-rate loans will probably suit you best. People who want to save money on the first few years of their loan and who are not afraid of a little risk will normally do better with an adjustable-rate loan.

> Beware of balloon loans. These are loans where you may pay interest only for a period of years and then have the entire principal balance come due in one lump-sum payment. If your financial future doesn't work out the way you expect it to, a loan with a balloon payment can destroy you.

ADJUSTABLE-RATE LOANS

Adjustable-rate loans are common, and they offer many advantages. As the name implies, the interest rates for adjustable-rate loans can and usually do fluctuate. The rates typically go up rather than down, but they can go down. There are many variations of adjustable-rate loans. Some are better than others.

Most adjustable-rate loans are adjusted annually, but others may adjust semi-annually or at other intervals. These loans are tied to specific indexes that affect how they are adjusted. Treasury bills are one of the common indexes.

Since lenders are not making long-term commitments for interest rates on adjustable loans, the starting interest rates are often very attractive. It would not be uncommon to find adjustable-rate loans with starting interest rates several points lower than fixed-rate loans. This can save you money in the early years of the loan.

Adjustable-rate loans that have annual and lifetime caps are safer than loans without caps. What are caps? The caps limit the amount of increase allowed in the interest rate of the loan. For example, if a loan has an annual cap of 2 percent, the interest rate cannot go up or down more than 2 percent in any given year. When the loan has a lifetime cap of 6 percent, the loan can never go up or down by more than 6 percent. For instance, if the loan had an interest rate of 6 percent when it was originated and the lifetime cap of the loan was 6 percent, the interest rate could never go higher than 12 percent.

Stay away from loans that have negative amortization. You could wind up owing more money after a year's worth of payments than you owed when you started making payments.

There are so many types of adjustable-rate loans available that each loan must be studied carefully. Avoid loans that don't have annual and lifetime caps, and avoid loans that allow negative amortization. With negative amortization your payments can be very low, but after paying on the loan for five years you may owe more than you borrowed. Negative amortization allows interest that is not being paid

Loans without caps are dangerous and should be avoided. There are no limits on how high the rates for these loans can go.

(to keep the payments low) to accrue, resulting in a higher loan balance than you started with.

IN-HOME FINANCING

Many contractors offer in-home financing plans. These plans are easy to apply for and are almost always approved if the applicant has equity in a home. There are many types of in-home financing plans. These plans typically charge a much higher interest rate than what a credit union or commercial bank would. However, points and closing costs are rarely an expensive factor with in-home financing.

> If you plan to sell your house within five years of completing your remodeling project, an adjustable-rate loan could be a real money-saver.

An in-home financing contract is similar in many ways to the financing offered by car dealers. There are times when this type of financing is worth considering, but normally you can do better by dealing with your bank or credit union.

FINANCE COMPANIES

Finance companies love to make second mortgages to home-owners with plenty of equity in their homes. The rates and terms offered by financing companies fluctuate, but they are rarely as good as rates available from credit unions and banks.

CONSULT YOUR ATTORNEY

Before you sign any financing agreement, it would be wise to consult your attorney. When you give a lender a mortgage against your home, the wrong words in the financing agreement could cause you to lose

> You will have to decide if you are willing to pay expensive legal rates to have potential financial agreements reviewed. Some home-owners choose to act on their own and save the money. What will you do? I would invest in a good attorney before I put my house on the line.

your house. While most banks use standard financing agreements, not all notes and mortgages are the same. When you are dealing with private financing from finance companies and in-home financing plans, you may run into some strange and undesirable language in the financing terms and agreement.

FINANCING FEES

Financing fees can add to the cost of your job. You know that the interest you pay on a loan over the coming years will increase the investment made in remodeling, but you may not be aware of some of the more immediate costs you may incur. Here are some examples of potential costs when obtaining financing:

- Loan application fees: Most lenders require you to pay a loan application fee when you apply for a loan. These fees are normally nonrefundable and vary in their amounts.

- Credit reporting fees: Credit reporting fees are also normally required at the time of loan application. These fees are rarely refundable, and their amounts also vary.

- Appraisal: When the loan you are applying for is a large one, the lender will normally require an appraisal of your property. The rules for when an appraisal is required vary from lender to lender, but if you are planning a complete kitchen-remodeling job, plan on the cost of an appraisal. Appraisal fees vary from location to location and lender to lender, but budget a few hundred dollars for the fee. A phone call to your intended lender will give you solid numbers to put into your budget.

- Points: When talking about financing, points are fees equal to 1 percent of the loan amount. In other words, if the loan amount is $20,000 and there is a fee of two points, the fee will be $400. These points are sometimes called origination fees, discount points, and prepaid interest.

- Title searches: Title searches are normally required when a house is being used as security for a loan. These searches reveal any outstanding liens or encumbrances that affect a homeowner's equity position. Fees for title searches also vary, but expect them to be a few hundred dollars.

- Surveys: If your kitchen or bathroom remodeling calls for adding space onto your home, expect to pay for a survey. A lender will want to be sure your addition is on your property and in compliance with zoning regulations. Surveys can cost only a few hundred dollars or they can cost much more, depending upon the size of your lot and the type of survey required by the lender.

- Other closing costs: There can be other closing costs that will have to be paid when you borrow for remodeling. These costs might include legal fees, filing fees, and other types of fees. Any reputable lender will provide you with an estimate of what your closing costs will be before you commit to a loan.

HOW MUCH WILL BORROWING MONEY ADD TO THE COST OF YOUR JOB?

How much will borrowing money add to the cost of your job? It will depend on where you borrow the money and what the individual lender charges, as well as what the interest rates are. You have just seen what some of the hidden costs might amount to, so now let's see how much the interest on a loan could cost you.

Assume that you are doing a major kitchen-remodeling job and that the amount of money borrowed from your bank will be $20,000. The interest rate is 10 percent, and the loan is a fixed-rate loan with a term of fifteen years. This means that you will make monthly payments of about $215 for 180 months. The total amount of these payments will be $38,700, nearly twice what you originally paid for the job. These kinds of numbers can be real eye-openers. Granted, a 10-percent rate is high today, but rates are likely to go up and this is merely an example.

Now let's look at the same job but with the money being borrowed from an in-home financing plan. The interest rate on this financing is 11.5 percent, and the rest of the terms are the same. Your payments for this loan will be about $234 a month. This doesn't sound like a big difference, but let's see what the total cost of the job is with this financing. The total amount of these payments will be $42,120, $3,420 more than with the bank financing.

> Before you borrow money, make sure you understand what you are signing and the monthly and total cost of your financing. This is one area of remodeling work where you don't want any surprises.

MAKING LOAN APPLICATIONS

Once you have decided to finance your job, you have to prepare for making a loan application. This is not a complicated process, but it helps to have all your documents in order. There will be many items a lender wants before approving your loan.

Getting a personal loan is a little different than getting a loan based on the value of the home improvements. You will need less documentation for a personal loan. As we look at your needs for a successful loan application, we will examine them on the assumption that the home improvements will be a factor in the loan approval. If you have plenty of equity in your home or a strong line of credit, you will not need all the items about to be discussed. Here are some of the requirements that you might expect when applying for financing:

- Plans and specifications: If a loan is being based on the value of an intended home improvement, the lender will want plans and specifications. He or she will review your plans and specs and will probably have a before-

Checklist of loan application needs

- ❑ Home address for the last five years
- ❑ Divorce agreements
- ❑ Child support agreements
- ❑ Social security numbers
- ❑ Two years of tax returns, if self-employed
- ❑ Paycheck stubs, if available
- ❑ Employee's tax statements (i.e., W-2, W-4)
- ❑ Gross income amount of household
- ❑ All bank account numbers, balances, names, and addresses
- ❑ All credit card numbers, balances, and monthly payments
- ❑ Employment history for last four years
- ❑ Information on all stocks or bonds owned
- ❑ Life insurance face amount and cash value
- ❑ Details of all real estate owned
- ❑ Rental income and expenses of investment property owned
- ❑ List of credit references with account numbers
- ❑ Financial statement of net worth
- ❑ Checkbook for loan application fees

Figure 10.2 Loan application needs.

and-after appraisal done on your home, based on the plans and specs you provide.

- Permits: Some lenders require all necessary permits to be purchased prior to closing a home-improvement loan. This assures the lender that the work may be done with the necessary code approvals.

- Tax returns: Some lenders want to see tax returns for the last two years. This normally is not required unless you are self-employed.

- Bank accounts: You will be asked to list all your bank accounts. Account numbers will be needed, and you must identify the type of accounts you have, such as checking and savings accounts.

- Financial statements: While you will not need a formal financial statement unless you are self-employed, you will have to list all your assets and liabilities. The liabilities will include credit-card debt, car loans, school loans, and any other financial obligations you have. Account numbers will be needed for each loan you have outstanding.

- Social Security numbers: Social Security numbers are required on loan applications, so if you don't know yours, find out what it is and bring it to loan application with you.

- Employment history: The loan application will request information about your employment history. If you have had different jobs in the last five years, be prepared to list the dates of your employment, the locations, your earnings, your supervisor, and the employers' addresses.

- Previous addresses: If you have lived at other addresses in the past few years, be prepared to provide detailed information.

- Credit references: There will be space on the loan application for listing credit references. When you list these references, you should be prepared to provide account numbers and addresses.

There may be a need for other information. For example, if you have been divorced, you may be required to provide a copy of the divorce decree. If you have had credit problems in the past, be prepared to explain in writing why you had trouble maintaining good credit.

LOAN APPROVAL

Once formal loan application is made, about all you can do is wait. The process can take as little as a week or as long as two months. You will normally be notified by mail when your loan is approved or denied.

Once the loan is approved, a closing date will be arranged. This will be the day you sign all the papers and receive the money to begin your project. Loan closings are usually simple procedures that take less than an hour to complete. However, you may wish to take your attorney to the closing with you. The papers you sign may affect your position of ownership in your home.

Now that all the preliminary work is out of the way, let's move on to the next chapter and get involved with the remodeling work.

11

Ripping Out Kitchens

The demolition process involved with remodeling a kitchen can be a major undertaking. Depending upon existing conditions and the degree of demolition needed, the job can consume days of your time. Not only can the demolition process be time-consuming, it can be dangerous for both you and your house. If you don't follow proper procedures, you may electrocute yourself or flood your home with water.

Should you do your own demolition work? If you are in good health and are handy, you shouldn't have any trouble completing your own demolition work. However, you should have an understanding for what is involved in the rip-out process before you begin gutting your kitchen. Here are some considerations to be aware of:

- There are safety hazards involved with demolition work.

- Eye protection should be worn at all times during the rip-out phase.

- Ear protection may be needed for some parts of a job.

- The proper clothing and footwear can reduce cuts, scratches, and punctures.

- There is a good chance some of your demolition work will be done while standing on a ladder, so caution must be exercised to avoid falling.

This book is not intended to teach you on-the-job safety procedures. There simply isn't room to discuss proper lifting procedures and other safety-related topics. But it is important to know that there are dangers involved with doing remodeling work. These dangers extend throughout a job. If you are not aware of how to work safely with tools, ladders, and general remodeling work, consult books on the subject of safety.

> Don't be too quick to start tearing a room apart. There is planning and preparation work needed before the actual work of ripping out a room should commence.

While I am not going to attempt to teach you safety procedures, I will show you some tricks of the trade. My many years of experience have allowed me to develop some techniques to make remodeling work easier, and I'm going to share these secrets with you. If you are ready to get down to some serious work, roll up your sleeves, and we will get started.

PREPARING FOR DEMOLITION

By preparing for demolition work in advance you can avoid a number of problems. One of the first problems inexperienced people run into with demolition work is the mess it makes in the rest of the home. There is a lot of dust and debris involved with demolition work, and keeping the mess contained in the room being ripped out is the first order of business.

Disposing of Debris

Before you can begin the containment process, you must have a plan for disposing of the debris you will create. If the room

Figure 11.1 During the demolition process, it may be hard to imagine the finished kitchen. *Courtesy of Armstrong*

being remodeled has a window or door that opens to the outside, you may be able to place a trash container near the opening and toss the debris out as you go along. This not only controls clutter in the workplace; it also makes the job go faster. If you have to pile the rubbish in the room and then haul it out to a trash container, you are handling the materials twice. Try to position a trash container where it is easily accessible and dispose of your refuse as you create it.

If you are working in a room that is on a second or third floor of your home, you may want to build a chute for your trash removal. Another option is to buy a tube that is used for pier foundations. This tube can be used as an enclosed chute and is relatively inexpensive. Set a trash container below the upstairs window where you will be discarding debris. Use framing lumber and plywood to build a trash chute if your job is not compatible with the cylindrical tube. The chute should have side rails that prevent debris from falling over the sides as

Using a debris chute or tube will reduce the amount of time and effort spent in getting debris out of the project room and into the trash pile or container.

it slides down to the trash container. The chute will resemble a sliding board. Have the chute extend from the trash container to the window and secure it firmly. With the chute in place, you can dump debris out the upstairs window and have it land safely in the container.

Dust Containment

Dust containment will be your next step in preparing for demolition. If you don't seal off the room you are remodeling from the rest of your home, dust will find its way into your carpeting and all over your home. The work involved in setting up dust containment is much easier than trying to deal with dust all over the home.

All you need for dust containment is some plastic and some duct tape. Seal all doors and other openings between the workspace and the remainder of the home with sheets of plastic. Cut the sheets larger than the openings you are covering and allow the plastic to extend several inches past the frame of the opening. Duct tape can be used to affix the plastic to the walls of the room you are working in. Keep the plastic on the side of the opening where you will be working, not on the side where the rest of your home is. Tape the plastic to the walls and floor using long strips of tape. Don't leave any portion of the seams untaped.

If you must use a door that opens into other living space for access to the room being remodeled, you may want to use an alternative method for sealing the opening. Since pulling tape loose from the walls and floor every time you want to enter or exit a room can be annoying, you might want to get a bit more creative.

Figure 11.2 Extensive demolition may be necessary to achieve the total look shown here. *Courtesy of Armstrong*

To avoid some hassles with coming and going, cut the sheet of plastic to be used for covering an entrance extra large. Tape the top and one side of the plastic to the walls in the way described above. Attach a 2 x 4 to the bottom of the plastic and roll the plastic around the piece of wood until the vertical fit is tight. The weight of the wood will hold the plastic down and eliminate the need for taping it to the floor.

On the remaining side of the opening, tape the plastic to the wall at the top, middle, and bottom, but don't use long strips of tape. Small pieces will do fine. There will be gaps along this edge of the plastic. Left alone, these gaps will allow dust to escape the room. To remedy the dust situation without sealing yourself in tightly, hang a second piece of plastic to overlap the lightly taped edge.

The second sheet of plastic should be taped to the wall at the top and along one edge with long strips of tape. The section of plastic that overlaps the other plastic should be taped at the top, middle, and bottom with the use of minimal tape. When this is done, the room is sealed, but you can come and go easily. All you have to do to open the exit is pull the tape from the bottom and middle section of the overlap and inner plastic. The bottom of the main covering will move easily when you push the wood to one side. This type of arrangement is effective in controlling dust while allowing reasonable ingress and egress to the space.

> If you have sensitive flooring, such as finished hardwood floors, cover them with construction paper to protect the finish. Failing to do this could result in scratches and scars if dust settles on the surface of the flooring.

RIPPING OUT A KITCHEN

What is involved in ripping out a kitchen? If you are taking the room down to bare studs and subfloor, there is a lot of work involved. You will have to work with plumbing and electrical devices, and you may have to work with part of your heating system. These mechanical systems must be treated with respect. The job will also involve removing wall coverings, ceilings, and floor coverings. While most homeowners have little problem with the demolition of a bathroom, there are some things to be careful of. Let's look at how the demolition process might go in an average bathroom.

Assume that you have your kitchen prepared for demolition and you are equipped with the proper safety precautions such as eye protection. In this job none of the existing fixtures will be salvaged. Where will you start the rip-out? The logical place to begin is with the plumbing fixtures.

Plumbing

Before you begin tearing out your old plumbing, make sure the water supply to the fixtures is cut off. Don't assume that a closed valve means that the water is off. Some valves fail with age. After you have closed the appropriate valves, test each fixture to see that the water is in fact shut off.

Begin by removing the kitchen sink. Once the sink is out and the plumbing is stabilized, you can move about the room as you wish. Wall cabinets, counters, base cabinets, and other features can now be removed. Check for the heating and air conditioning requirements. Look at the electrical needs. Concentrate on the sensitive issues, which include the plumbing, heating, electrical, and air-conditioning elements.

> Taking a hammer to an enameled kitchen sink can be dangerous. The finish on the sink can break and fly about the room. Without protective clothing and equipment, you can be cut by the flying china

A hammer works well in removing the walls. Don't cut into the walls blindly with a saw. You might hit live electrical wires. Beat holes in the walls with a hammer and pull the wall covering off. If you have your heart set on using a saw, at least open the walls with a hammer and check for wiring and plumbing before using it.

> Don't use a saw to cut into walls. There may be live electrical wires in the wall. Beat a hole in the wall with a hammer to inspect for wiring before using a saw on the wall.

When you have the walls stripped to the bare studs, you have much of the demo work done. There is still the ceiling to take down. Do it the same way that you did the walls. Stay focused. Mistakes happen when people rush around. Demo work can be hard work, but the techniques are fairly easy.

Heating

You may not have to do much with the heating system in your kitchen. If your heat comes in through ducts in the floor, all you have to do is remove the register from the duct and protect the open duct from falling debris. You can stuff a towel in the duct or cut a piece of plywood to cover the opening.

Figure 11.3 When the rip-out process seems too disruptive, just remember that you will soon enjoy working in your new kitchen. *Courtesy of Armstrong*

If you have hot-water baseboard heat, you will want to remove the baseboard-heating element. This will require shutting down the boiler and may require draining the heating system. If you are working on the top floor of your home, you shouldn't need to drain much water from the heating system before cutting the supply and return pipes at the baseboard unit. However, if there is heat installed in rooms above your kitchen, drain the heating system to a point below the kitchen.

There will be removable end-caps on the baseboard-heating unit. Remove these caps by pulling them off to reveal the supply and return pipes. The pipes should be copper. If they are, they can be cut with a hacksaw or a pipe cutter. Once the pipes are cut,

If you have an old house that is equipped with radiators, try to avoid removing them. Old radiators can become damaged when moved, and they are hard and expensive to replace.

remove the screws that hold the baseboard unit to the wall and remove the heating unit.

Electrical

Now that the plumbing and heating are out of the way, you are ready to work with electrical devices and fixtures. Turn off the power to the kitchen. If you are going to remove your own electrical fixtures, be certain the electricity to the wires is off. Use an electrical meter to test each wire before working with it. If you don't know how to use an electrical meter, you have no business working with electricity. Call in a professional.

With the power turned off, remove all cover plates from switches and outlets. Remove the globes or shades on your lights and the light bulbs. Most electrical fixtures are attached to their electrical boxes with threaded rod and nuts. Remove these nuts and the fixture should come loose. Remove the wire nuts (plastic covers protecting the wires) and test for electricity.

> Don't attempt to work with electricity if you are not absolutely certain that you have the ability to do so. One mistake with electrical work can be the last one you will ever make in life.

When you are sure the power is off, separate the fixture wires from the house wiring. Install wire nuts on the house wiring and tuck it back into the electrical box.

If you have electric baseboard heat, it should be attached to the wall with screws. Before handling the wiring to the heat, make sure the electricity is off. You cannot assume that all your bathroom wiring is on the same circuit. Just because the light doesn't have power coming to it doesn't mean the heat is safe to work with.

Walls And Ceilings

Removing finished walls and ceilings is not difficult if you are working with drywall. Use a hammer to open the walls and ceiling and to expose all wiring, plumbing, and heating. A dust mask will help protect you from the massive amounts of dust this process will create. You can then either continue to demo the walls and ceiling with a hammer or you can cut the drywall out with a saw. Window and door trim will also have to be removed during this stage.

If your walls are made of plaster, you have a lot more work in front of you. A reciprocating saw is the fastest way to cut through plaster and the lathe behind it. However, use a hammer to open sections of the wall before running the saw through the plaster. It is easy to cut wires and plumbing by accident.

Flooring

Removing vinyl flooring is not difficult. Start by removing all baseboard trim and shoe molding. When the molding is removed, the edges of the flooring will be exposed. You may be able to grasp the ends and pull the flooring up. If the floor is difficult to remove, you can use a floor scraper to remove it.

If you are removing a ceramic tile floor, you can chisel the tiles up or break them out with a hammer. Remember to protect your eyes and body from the sharp slivers created by breaking the tile.

Odds and Ends

There will be some odds and ends to tend to. Go around the kitchen and remove all existing nails that protrude from the walls and ceiling. Sweep the floor and scrape it until it is clean. Cap all pipes to keep debris from entering them. Make sure all electrical wires are protected with wire nuts. Look around and tidy up any loose ends.

When you are involved with remodeling you are sure to run into some unexpected conditions. You might find that your sub-floor and even your floor joists have been damaged by water leaks. When you open a wall, you might come face to face with a nest of angry bees. There are all sorts of things that can disrupt your remodeling plans. You have to prepare for any number of unexpected events. This is what keeps the work exciting.

12

Unexpected Conditions

It is very likely that you will run into some unexpected existing conditions when you begin remodeling your kitchen. You can plan and plan for a perfect job, but you cannot always plan for the unexpected. However, if you know what types of unexpected conditions may exist, you can hedge your odds for success.

Professionals are sometimes plagued with problems with existing conditions. It might be that the water pipes to a kitchen sink froze at some time and swelled to a point where fittings will not slide over them. The problem could be a wall that is not plumb or a floor that is not level. When you are installing kitchen cabinets, it is very important to have level floors and plumb walls to work with.

While most of the unexpected problems that arise have to do with building materials and conditions, it is not unusual for other types of problems to pop up from time to time. When you open an existing wall, you never know what you might find. There could be a nest of bees hiding behind the drywall or an angry rodent. If you remove the ceiling in a kitchen that has its own attic, you may be surprised to see a swarm of bats flying about, startled by your actions. Crawling under the house to work on the plumbing might bring you face to face with a snake or feral cat. Without doubt there are plenty of opportunities for surprises when remodeling.

Some of the wildlife stories you have just heard about may be difficult to believe, but I have had all these things happen to me. I have run into skunks, rattlesnakes, rats, squirrels, feral cats, bats, bees, porcupines, and other types of wildlife during my remodeling career. Most of the encounters ended amicably, but some of them were exciting for a while. I tell you this not to scare you but to prepare you. If you are aware of what you might find at different stages of your job, you will be better prepared to deal with the problems.

To elaborate on what you might expect during your remodeling experience, let's look at the various phases of your job and see what might get in your way.

FLOORS

When you are working with your floors, you may find that the subfloor or floor joists must be replaced. The damaged floor structure may not be evident until you have removed the finish floor covering. Water damage is a frequent cause of this type of problem, but it could result from termites or other wood-infesting insects. The floor joists may simply have rotted to a point where they are no longer structurally sound.

WALLS AND CEILINGS

Walls and ceilings can conceal all types of potential problems. When the area cavities behind finished walls and ceilings are exposed, you may find that the insulation has become dilapidated or was never installed. This can add to your work with unexpected labor and material costs.

Bees and snakes often take up residency in hollow walls. It can be very unnerving to cut out a wall section and be swarmed by angry bees. Seeing a big snake slither out of sight in the wall can ruin your whole day. You never know when the snake will turn up again.

The walls studs could be covered with the telltale signs of termites. Not only will you have damaged studs to replace, you will be faced with the expense of professional termite treatments.

The bottom plate of your wall may have rotted, causing much more extensive work to the wall than you expected.

Removing a ceiling can reveal water damage to the floor above you. There are many times when leaking plumbing fixtures and water damage go undetected until a ceiling is removed.

Removing a ceiling that has an attic above it can cover you in insulation. Most attics have insulation lying between the joists on the backside of the ceiling you are working with. Cutting out a section of this type of ceiling and getting a face full of loose insulation is no fun.

When removing a ceiling, protect yourself from falling debris. It is common for loose-fill insulation to come pouring out of ceilings that have attic space above them. Eye protection and a dust mask will help to prevent complications from this type of work.

Attics can be home to a number of wild inhabitants. Bats, birds, snakes, rats, mice, squirrels, and even raccoons can be found in attics. Imagine your surprise if you are dropping a ceiling and confront a curious raccoon. If the ceiling you are working with has an attic above it, attempt to inspect the attic prior to opening the ceiling.

MECHANICAL SYSTEMS

Mechanical systems can cause much frustration. You may think you are working with copper plumbing pipes only to discover that they are brass. Old brass pipe can be cut with standard copper cutters, but copper fittings will not normally slide over the brass pipe. You might find that the electrical wiring in your kitchen was run in a haphazard way and that some wires are dead while others are hot. This can be a shocking experience.

Most mechanical problems can be overcome with minimal trouble, but some of them are serious. For example, you may discover that your toilet was not mounted to a flange and that the pipe connecting to the toilet was an old-fashioned lead bend. If this is the case, your main drainage system is old enough to be made from cast-iron pipe, and converting it to plastic pipe will require a special soil pipe cutter.

If you relocate a radiator that provides heat to your room, you may find that it leaks when you reinstall it. This can be expensive to correct, not to mention frustrating.

CABINETS

Installing cabinets is very difficult if you do not have level floors and plumb walls to work with. You can spend many hours installing shims to get the cabinets to fit properly. If you don't take the time to level the cabinets, the doors and drawers are not likely to work smoothly.

Check the walls early on in your job to see that they are plumb. Walls that are not plumb will result in gaps where counters or cabinets sit against the walls. It is far better to deal with walls that are out of plumb before you attempt to make new installations.

COUNTERTOPS

When you install your new countertop, you may discover that your walls are very much out of plumb. The top will be tight against the wall at one point but have a gap at another. If you don't know that the wall is out of plumb until you install the countertop, the cost of your job will go up considerably. If the gap is significant, you will have to remove the finished wall covering and use furring strips to build the wall out or order a new countertop. Either way you are going to lose time and money.

UNDER THE HOUSE

If you have to crawl under your house during your project, you may find any number of unexpected problems. Your floor joists could be riddled with holes from powder post beetles. Water could be standing under the home, creating mold and rotting your wood. While you are under your home, look for any defects that might exist. You may not want to fix them, but it is better to fix them before the problem escalates.

After you have successfully completed the demolition phase of your remodeling, it is time to start putting it all back together again. Unlike trying to put Humpty Dumpty back together again, you won't need all the King's men and all the King's horses to put your kitchen back together. You may need some help from friends or contractors, but the job is manageable.

The task of restoring your kitchen will go much more smoothly if you do it in an organized manner. There will be a lot of work to do, and some of the work will be much more difficult

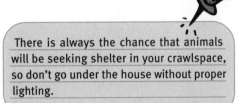

It is embarrassing to have a freshly remodeled kitchen and new appliances that will not fit in the openings you provided for them. A mere ¼ inch can keep you from getting a new refrigerator into its opening, so verify the dimensions of all appliances before creating space for them. The same advice applies to fixtures.

There is always the chance that animals will be seeking shelter in your crawlspace, so don't go under the house without proper lighting.

Anticipating what you are doing and thinking is the best way to avoid serious problems. If you consider what could be inside a wall or under a floor, you are less likely to experience trouble with your remodeling. For example, failure to think about wires that are installed in a wall could cause you to cut them with a saw. This could result in an electrical shock, and it will certainly result in additional work. Think before you act, and you will have a good chance of getting through your job with minimal interference.

if it is not done in the right sequence. For example, should you install your countertop before or after you paint your walls? Most contractors paint first and then install countertops.

Why do they do it in this order? If the counter is installed first, there will be no paint on the wall behind the counter. This means the painter will have to paint right up to the edge of the counter. Painting the room will be much more difficult with the cabinets and countertops installed. Access to the walls will not be as good, and there is always a risk of spilling paint on expensive cabinets and counters.

Some professionals and many homeowners believe countertops should be installed before a room is painted. Why? Because they think that freshly painted walls are likely to be dinged when the counters are installed. It is probable that some scuffing will occur on the walls, but it is much easier to touch up a few dings with the counter in place than it is to paint all the walls with the counter in the way. This is only one example of how the proper planning and scheduling can make your job run more smoothly. Let's look ahead now to some of the other ways you can improve your efficiency in remodeling.

CREATE A PRODUCTION SCHEDULE

Before you begin your work, create a production schedule. Organize all the work that will need to be done into a logical progression. Break the work down into phases, such as rough-in plumbing and final plumbing. It is unlikely that your schedule will work out exactly the way you design it, but by having it in writing you will be less likely to overlook work that needs to be done, and you have a better chance of keeping the job on track.

Once you have a list of all the types of work required in your job, assign dates to each task. For example, you might schedule rough plumbing for June 10 and rough electrical work for June 11. Remember to allow time for code inspections. Some phases of your job will not be able to progress until other phases are inspected and approved. For example, you could not hang drywall and conceal rough plumbing and electrical work until inspection approval has been given.

When you have tentative dates by all your work phases, note the work that will be done for you by contractors. This will enable you to give them plenty of advance notice of when their services will be required. If part of the job doesn't go according to schedule, remember to change the dates for all aspects of the work that will be affected.

It may take several attempts before you have revised your production schedule to a point where it is reasonably accurate. If you will be using contractors, ask them to provide estimates for the amount of time they will need to complete their work.

It is unlikely that you will know how much time to allow for the various types of work. If you are doing all the work yourself, the exact timing will not be as critical as it might with contractors. However, even if you are doing the work yourself, you must develop a rough idea of when various phases will be complete. Otherwise you will not be able to project the dates for ordering cabinets, countertops, and other supplies.

LAY YOUR PRODUCTION SCHEDULE OUT IN LOGICAL ORDER

It is important that you lay your production schedule out in logical order. Since you are not an experienced general contractor or remodeler, you are not likely to know what a logical order is. Don't worry—you are about to find out. All time estimates are based on professional work. You should adjust the times to compensate for your skill levels.

Check with your suppliers to determine how much advance notice is required to have various items delivered when you want them.

Preparation

Preparation work is the first phase of any remodeling job. This is when you make arrangements for trash removal and dust control. Permits are often obtained at this stage of the job. The preparation work can usually be completed in a day.

Demolition

Demolition work is the next step in remodeling a kitchen. However, before you begin tearing out what you have, order the materials to put the space back together again. Check with your suppliers to determine how much advance notice is required to have various items delivered when you want them. For example, you can probably get a load of lumber in a day or two, but it could take weeks to get new cabinets.

Demolition work for a kitchen can often take two or three days to strip down to the bare studs and subfloor. The extra cabinets require additional time to remove. You have to remove appliances and related equipment before the rip-out is done.

Rough Framing

If you are relocating or adding walls in your remodeling job, now is the time to do it. Framing work often requires a building permit and an inspection. If you are planning to install underlayment on your subfloor, do it while you are in the rough-framing phase. Most framing for kitchen remodeling can be completed in a day or two.

Plumbing

Once the demo work is done, it is time to make any adjustments needed in the rough plumbing. If you are installing new kitchen fixtures, this is the time to do it. This work usually requires a permit and inspection. The rough plumbing for a kitchen rarely takes more than a day to complete.

Heating

Heating work is normally done after plumbing and prior to electrical work. You may need a permit and inspection for the heating work required in your job. The heating work required for a typical kitchen remodeling job will take no more than a day.

Electrical

Electrical work typically follows plumbing and heating work. Again, a permit and inspection may be required. This work should be completed in one day.

Insulation

If you have any insulation work to be done, it should be done after the plumbing, heating, and electrical work has been done and inspected. Many code jurisdictions require insulation to be inspected prior to concealment. The building permit obtained for the job covers insulation work. Installing insulation doesn't take long, but allow a day for it in your production schedule. Jobs don't run as smoothly when different trades are on the job on the same day.

Drywall

Once all your mechanical work and insulation are installed and inspected, you are ready for drywall. This work is covered under the building permit, but it often requires an inspection. Rarely will there be a specific drywall inspection, but the work will be examined when the final building inspection is done.

Before drywall seams are sanded, be sure that you have dust-containment procedures in place. The fine dust from the sanding will invade all the nooks and crannies of your home without proper containment.

After the drywall is hung and taped, it will need to be finished. This is a lengthy process, since it requires days during which you will be unable to do much of anything else. Three coats of joint compound are typically installed on new drywall seams, corners, and dimples. Each coat of compound must dry and be sanded before the next layer is applied. The sanding is very dusty work.

Drywall can be hung on the walls and ceiling of a room in a day. The taping and first coat of compound can also be installed on the first day. By the second day, the second coat of compound can usually be applied. By the beginning of the fourth day, the walls and ceiling should be ready for paint.

Painting

The next phase of work to have done is the painting. Generally at least a primer coat and one coat of paint are used, and this work will take at least two days. Most professionals apply two coats of primer and two coats of paint.

Finish Flooring

Finish flooring is normally done next. This part of the job doesn't require a special inspection, and it should be completed in a day.

Protect new flooring once it is installed. Some contractors apply a layer or two of construction paper for protection. When possible it can be desirable to cover the flooring with cardboard or some other protective material. A favorite of mine is a thin, inexpensive carpet pad. I place the pad over the new flooring and then seal the area with plastic or paper.

Cabinets, Counters, and Fixtures

The cabinets, counters, and fixtures can be installed after the finish flooring is in. Individual inspections are not required for this work. These items will be inspected when all final inspections are done.

A good kitchen crew can hang and set all the cabinets in a standard kitchen in a day, but you should allow them at least two days for the job. Professional plumbers can set all the fixtures for a kitchen in less than a day. Electricians and heating mechanics can be in and out in a day when setting fixtures.

Trim Work

Once all the cabinets and fixtures are in, the trim work can be done. Some people install trim before fixtures and cabinets are installed, and others do it afterwards. Either way will work, but I prefer to have the trim installed afterwards. It always seems to fit better that way.

Most professionals paint or stain their trim before they install it. Then all that is required, once the trim is in place, is filling nail holes and touch-up work on the paint or stain. Installing trim can be time-consuming, but any good professional can trim a kitchen in a day.

Final Touches

There will be many small final touches to do before the job can be considered finished. These odds and ends can take a day or two to complete.

Cleaning Up

Cleaning up the mess and the new fixtures will be the last phase in the work. This should take less than a day.

Final Inspections

Once the job is completely finished, you are ready for your final inspections. This may involve a visit from a plumbing inspector, electrical inspector, HVAC inspector, and building inspector.

Some jobs will require work not mentioned in this outline, such as tile work or decorative stenciling. This list of work should give you a good idea of how to plan your production schedule. There is little doubt that you will have to make adjustments for the time allocations, but with some advance planning and effort you can make your job run smoother with a production schedule.

13

Flooring

The floor of your kitchen is a focal point of the room. The right floor coverings can distinguish the room and make a statement about its owner. The wrong floor covering can darken the room or give an unbalanced appearance. Your choice in a finished floor covering will have a strong effect on the overall appearance of your remodeled room.

Even with the best-finished floor covering available, bad subflooring and floor joists can prohibit your room from being outstanding. If the floor squeaks every time you walk across it, you will notice the squeak more than you will the attractive floor covering. If the joists are weak and the floor is spongy, you may wonder when your refrigerator is going to fall through the floor.

Most of the work done in routine kitchen remodeling is not of a structural nature, but the flooring is. While you need superior carpentry skills to build a kitchen cabinet on a custom level, you may not need them to repair damaged floor joists. It is not common to discover rotted or damaged floor joists, but it does happen. What would you do if you removed water-stained subflooring and found the tops of three floor joists rotted to a point where the point of a pencil would penetrate them? A lot of people would panic and assume the joist would have to be removed and replaced. It is possible that the joists would need replacement, but it is more likely that a little repair job could solve the problem.

This chapter is going to show you many aspects of your flooring system. You will learn about floor joists, subflooring, underlayment, and finished floor coverings. There will be tips on how to handle rotten joists the easy way, and how to get the bubbles out of your new vinyl flooring. If you are ready, let's get on with an in-depth study of floors.

FLOOR JOISTS

Floor joists are the structural members that support the subfloor. They are normally boards with dimensions ranging from 2 x 8 inches to 2 x 12 inches. Floor joists span the distances between outside walls and support girders. The length of the span and the use of the floor influence the size of the joist.

> Never skimp on the size of floor joists. If you are dealing with a span that is a borderline case between the minimum size required and the next larger, go with the larger joist.

If you remove your subfloor and find a few of the floor joists to be rotted, you may not have to replace them. It is entirely possible that you can add new supports without removing the old ones. In many cases all you will have to do is slide new joists in place on each side of the damaged one and nail them to it. The new joists should be the same length and have the same dimensions as the old joist. This is normally not a very difficult procedure and it works fine in most circumstances.

If only a small section of a joist is damaged, you may be able to get by with scabbing new pieces of wood on the old joist. Assume that an existing joist was damaged, but only for about 2 feet of its length. You may be able to attach new wood on each

Figure 13.1 Nothing matches the beauty of a hardwood floor. *Courtesy of Armstrong*

side of the damaged area to avoid installing complete joists. The scab wood should extend well past the damaged area. In this case about 4 feet in length should be sufficient. This practice may not be suitable in all situations. Check with your local building inspector before relying on this type of repair.

Another option available for joists with small areas of damage is a process in which the old joist is headed off. To head off a joist, you cut out the damaged section. Then joist-size material is used to span the distance between sound joists. The cut end of the damaged joist is attached to the new wood that is running perpendicular to the cut end. This procedure is also used when an opening is needed between floor joists for the passage of a chimney or stairs.

SUBFLOORING

Subflooring is the flooring that attaches to floor joists. It can be made of boards, but it is usually made with sheets of plywood

Figure 13.2   Modern wood floors are specially treated to deal with the demands of families and their pets. *Courtesy of Armstrong*

or particleboard. Most jurisdictions allow two options when installing subflooring. Either one layer of tongue-and-groove material or two layers of standard plywood or particleboard may be used. It is not normally acceptable to install a single layer of material that is not fitted with a tongue-and-groove installation.

UNDERLAYMENT

Underlayment is usually a thin (about ¼ inch) sheet of plywood that is laid over a subfloor. The underlayment is normally sanded on one side and provides a smooth surface for the installation of finish flooring.

VINYL FLOORING

Vinyl flooring is the most common type of flooring used in kitchens. It is generally available in widths of 6 or 12 feet. Vinyl flooring can be tricky to install, but the job can be done by anyone with average skills and patience.

Before you start installing your new vinyl, make sure the area of the installation is clean and smooth. The surface should be flat and without cracks, depressions, or bulges. Cracks in floors can be filled with special compounds. These filling compounds are available from the same stores that sell flooring.

Before installing your floor, roll the flooring up with the finish side facing outward. Leave it in this position for a full day. Maintain an even temperature of about 65 degrees F in the room where the vinyl is being stored.

> Don't attempt to install vinyl flooring when it is cold. The material will be difficult to work with, and it may be brittle.

If your floor is going to require seams, make them before installing the flooring. Lay two pieces of flooring in place so

Figure 13.3   Examples of vinyl sheet flooring. *Courtesy of Armstrong*

that they overlap. Make sure the pattern meets and matches. Using a straightedge and a utility knife, cut through both pieces of flooring where the seam will be made. Remove the scrap flooring and attach the two pieces of finish flooring to the floor at the seam. Use a hand roller to press the flooring down. The back of the flooring should be in contact with the adhesive or tape you are using for the installation. Cover the seam with a sealing compound.

> Vinyl flooring should be laid out in a room with enough excess vinyl that the flooring rolls up on the walls. A utility knife is one of the best tools to cut vinyl flooring with.

> When you are securing your flooring to the subfloor, you may use adhesive, tape, staples, or a combination.

A floor roller should be used to roll wrinkles out of a new installation. Rollers can be rented at tool centers. When the vinyl is flat, cut away excess flooring. Run a utility knife along a straightedge to cut the vinyl where it meets the walls. Baseboard or shoe molding will then be installed to hide the joint between the floor and wall.

CARPET

Carpet is not a common floor covering for kitchens, but it is sometimes used. If after careful consideration you decide to install carpeting in your kitchen, make sure the pile of the carpet faces the entrance. This will enhance the appearance of your room. Most carpet is available in widths up to 12 feet.

> If you want to install carpeting in your kitchen, weigh the pros and cons. While carpeting makes the floor warmer and less slippery than vinyl or tile, it retains moisture and that can create problems with mold, mildew, and rot.

The installation of loop-pile and cut-pile carpeting can be done by homeowners, but you will probably have to rent a few tools. You will also have to be careful in your measurements and cuts.

Most carpet is held in place by tackless strips. These strips are normally about four feet long and have sharp teeth that bite into the carpet. Tackless strips come in different sizes. Check with your carpet supplier for the proper size to use with your carpet and pad.

A rule-of-thumb distance between a tackless strip and a wall is a gap equal to two-thirds the thickness of the carpet.

The tackless strips are installed around the perimeter of the area to be carpeted. Doorways and cased openings are fitted with metal trim strips. These strips are either folded over or nailed on top of the carpet to give a finished edge that people will not trip over.

Tackless strips should be installed at a uniform distance from the wall. Check with your carpet supplier for the proper distance to maintain between the edge of the strip and the wall.

The carpet pad is installed within the boundaries of the tackless strips, but it is not attached to the strips. Check the manufacturer's recommendations to determine which side of the pad should face the subfloor. Carpet pads are usually stapled to the subfloor.

Carpeting should be unrolled, flattened out, and stored at room temperature before it is cut. When you do cut the carpet, leave at least 3 inches of extra carpet in all directions.

If you are working with a cut-pile carpet, cut it from the back. Take measurements and use a utility knife, along with a chalk line or straightedge, to make an even cut along the carpet backing. Loop-pile carpet should be cut from the finished side rather than on the backing.

Carpet installation requires the use of a tool that stretches the carpet. There are knee-kickers and power stretchers available for this part of the job, and both types of tools can be rented at most tool centers.

Carpet that must be seamed should be seamed before it is stretched. Two pieces of carpet should overlap each other by about 1 inch at the seam. Make sure the pile of both pieces of carpet is running in the same direction. Use a row-running knife to cut a straight line along the edge of the overlapped carpet. The knife will cut both pieces of carpet simultaneously.

When the cut is complete, remove the cut strip from beneath the top piece of carpet. Lay both edges back to expose the subfloor. Install a strip of hot-melt seaming tape on the subfloor. The tape should be laid so that the center of the tape is in line with the center point where the two pieces of carpet will meet.

Run a hot iron over the seaming tape to activate it. Heat only small sections at a time, and maintain an iron temperature of about 250 degrees F. When the tape becomes sticky, roll the edges of the carpet into place and butt them together. Continue this process, in small sections, until the complete seam is made.

To stretch carpet, you should have both a knee-kicker and a power stretcher. The stretching process is normally started in a corner. Using the knee-kicker, attach the carpet to the tackless strips on two walls at the corners.

After the first corner is secured, use a power stretcher to secure the corner directly opposite the one already done. Power stretchers have the ability to telescope to long lengths and can span an entire room.

Knee-kickers are used to secure carpet between previously secured locations. Basically, two walls are done with the knee-kicker and two walls are done with the power stretcher.

When the carpet is attached to tackless strips, cut away excess carpet with a utility knife. Then use a flat-bit screwdriver to tuck remaining carpet into the gap between the tack strip and the wall.

Carpet at doorways and openings should be cut to size, and a metal strip should be installed on top. If you are using a metal strip that must be bent over the carpeting, use a wide block of wood and a hammer to drive the metal strip down tight. The wooden block should be placed over the strip and tapped down with the hammer. Do not hit the strip with just a hammer. The strip will be damaged. If you are using a nail-on strip, put the metal in place and tack it down.

CERAMIC TILE

Ceramic tile is often found in kitchens. If you decide to use tile, you will have plenty of choices to choose from. Tile floors can be made of quarry tile, mosaic tile, and glazed ceramic tile. Quarry tile comes in large squares, and it is produced in natural clay colors. Mosaic tile is small and generally comes with numerous tiles connected to a single backing. Glazed ceramic tile may be bought as squares or rectangles.

> When installing tile, the choice of which type of adhesive to use is often determined by the manufacturer's recommendations. Check with your tile dealer for specifics. Always follow the manufacturer's recommendations.

Underlayment should be installed over a subfloor before the tile is installed. The underlayment should be at least ⅜ inch thick and should be installed with ⅛-inch expansion gaps between the sheets. The tile can be secured with adhesives. The adhesive may be organic or epoxy. Epoxy is the preferred adhesive for floors where dampness is a problem.

Grout material is a product that fills the gaps between tiles, preventing water and dirt from collecting in the voids. There are numerous types of grout material. Check with your tile dealer before selecting a grout material.

Proper planning is a critical element of good tile installations. Deciding how to obtain the proper pattern and spacing will require thought. Special saws and cutters should be used to cut your tiles. These saws and cutters can be rented at tool centers.

Installation methods vary. You should check with your dealer and follow the manufacturer's recommendations for the installation of your tile. Let's look at one common way of installing tile.

Figure 13.4   Examples of ceramic tile. *Courtesy of Armstrong*

Trowel adhesive on the underlayment to a thickness of about ¼ inch. Use plastic spacers (available at tile dealers) to maintain even spacing between your tiles. Lay your first tile in the center of the floor and lay subsequent tiles out from that point.

As you set the tiles in the adhesive, press them down firmly. If needed, a rubber hammer can be used to tap the tile into place. Use a long level to check the consistency of the floor. The tile should be installed level. After the tile is set, you must wait for the adhesive to dry.

When the adhesive is dry, you are ready to grout the tile. The grouting should be spread over the floor, filling all gaps between the tiles. This is usually done with a special trowel.

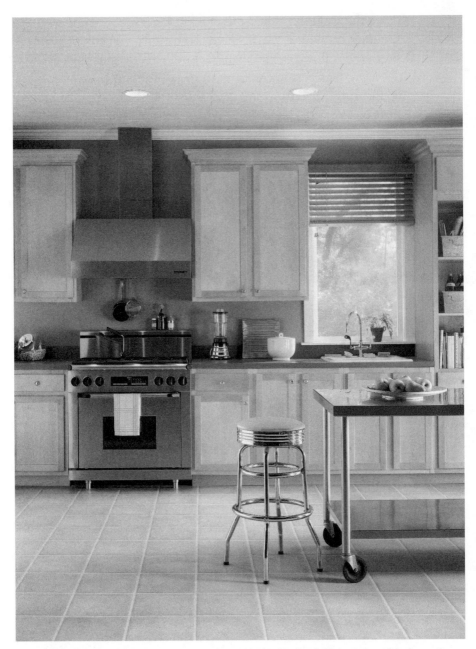

Figure 13.5   Durable ceramic tile enhances the look of this modern kitchen. *Courtesy of Armstrong*

Once the grout has filled the cracks, wash the remainder of the grouting off with a wet sponge. To be sure you install your tile properly, follow the tile manufacturer's recommendations.

Now that you know how to install the most popular types of flooring for bathrooms and kitchens, let's move on to the next chapter and learn about walls and ceilings.

14

Walls and Ceilings

Walls and ceilings can account for much of the work required in remodeling a room. If finished walls are not removed, the work may only entail painting. But major remodeling often involves building new walls and recovering old walls. Under these conditions the effort required is considerable, and skills in many trades are needed.

You may be faced with framing new interior partitions or installing a new door or window. Insulation may need to be added to the exterior walls, and getting a good finish on drywall is something of an art. Even painting is not always as easy as it looks. This chapter is going to introduce you to the work that may be involved with your walls and ceilings.

FRAMING

Framing work is often called rough carpentry, but that doesn't mean you can use rough estimates or get by with rough skills. If the framing is not done properly, the rest of the job will suffer. For example, if you frame a new wall to hang cabinets on and the wall is out of plumb, you are going to have a tough time hanging the cabinets in a satisfactory manner. Some kitchen remodeling jobs don't require any framing work, but others do. Framing interior partitions is not difficult, but there are a few tricks of the trade that makes the job easier. Let's see what they are.

Building a Wall

When you are building a wall, you can get the job done in several ways. Most professionals build walls by laying the framing on the subfloor and then standing the walls up. This process allows you to frame the entire wall under comfortable circumstances.

Before you start driving nails, lay out the wall locations on the subfloor. Mark the wall location with a chalk line. Once the wall location is known, measure the length of the proposed wall. This will tell you how long your top and bottom (sole) plates should be.

Carpenters normally use one 2-x-4-inch stud as a bottom plate and two studs for the top plate of a wall. Begin by cutting the bottom and top plates to the desired length. Next, measure to determine the length needed for vertical studs. Remember to allow for the thickness of your top and bottom plates when measuring between the ceiling joists and the subfloor. After you are sure of your measurements, cut the wall studs to the desired length.

When building walls that will meet at corners, you have to have a way to tie the two wall sections together. This is normally done with studs that are turned flat in the wall section. This provides a solid surface to attach to. You can screw or nail one wall section to the other in this manner.

Turn the bottom and top plates over on their edges. Place the first wall stud at one end of the plates and nail it into place. Do the same with a second stud at the other end. You have created a rectangle, and all you have to do is install the additional wall studs. Studs are normally installed so that there are

Figure 14.1 Wood paneling on the walls creates a cozy country kitchen. *Courtesy of Wellborn Cabinet, Inc.*

16 inches from the center of one stud to the center of another. When the wall section is complete, you can stand it up and nail it into place.

WINDOWS AND DOORS

Your framing work may involve for windows and doors. It is not uncommon for new windows and doors to be installed during large remodeling jobs. Let's take a look at the types of windows and doors you might want to use and how to frame for them. Here are some of your options:

- Casement windows are well known for their energy-efficient qualities. This style of window offers the advantage of full airflow. When you crank out a casement window, the entire window opens.

- Double-hung windows are the type of windows found in most homes. These windows are generally less expensive than casement windows, and they are well accepted as an industry standard.

- Skylights can give a kitchen plenty of natural light. Rooms filled with sunshine generally appear larger and more inviting. Today's skylights are available with built-in shades and screens.

- Metal doors are relatively inexpensive, and they can be equipped with good insulation qualities. These doors are available as solid doors, stamped doors that give the appearance of a six-panel door, and half glass doors, with or without grids. These doors can be painted, but they cannot be stained.

- Wood doors typically cost more than metal doors, but they are available in more styles. Some people don't like wood doors because they can warp and become hard to operate.

Figure 14.2 Casement windows by the window seat are a beautiful enhancement. *Courtesy of Wellborn Cabinet, Inc.*

- French doors are a wonderful way to brighten up an eat-in kitchen. These doors are beautiful, but they tend to be expensive.

FRAMING WINDOW AND DOOR OPENINGS

Framing window and door openings is simple when building new walls, but it can be complicated if you are cutting new windows or doors into existing walls. Your work will affect the siding on your home and the structural integrity of the exterior wall. The basics of framing window and door openings are about to be explained, but understand that existing conditions at your home may call for professional help in this phase of the project.

A typical window frame will involve jack studs, cripple studs, and a header. The header will provide strength and support for whatever is sitting on top of the wall. It is usually made with lumber that is nailed together. Jack studs are installed under the header to support it. A horizontal board is installed below the header at a distance equal to the rough-opening dimension for the window being installed. This board is nailed to the wall studs and supported with short studs from below. The area above the header is filled with cripple studs. These cripples extend from the header to the top plate, completing the window frame.

Don't install headers that are too small. The headers carry weight and must be large enough to get the job done. It may be tempting to use leftover wood. Don't do it. Build your headers out of wood with the proper dimensions for the application.

The rough door opening should extend all the way to the subfloor. A header, jack studs, and upper cripples will be installed in a manner very similar to window framing. However, the lower framing that is done with a window is eliminated, and the section of the bottom wall plate that runs

Framing for an exterior door is similar to framing for windows. Most doors are available as pre-hung units. These units come to the job ready for installation. It makes sense to buy pre-hung door units. The time saved offsets the additional cost.

through the door opening is cut out. Cripple studs may not be used when a large header is installed.

WINDOW INSTALLATION

If you have framed your rough opening properly, window installation is simple. Many windows have nailing flanges for attaching the window unit to the frame walls. Set the window unit in the rough opening and make sure it is plumb. Nail the unit in place by driving nails through the flange. The flange should be on the exterior side of the house. If you are working with windows that don't have flanges, you will be nailing through the window framing.

DOOR INSTALLATION

When you are working with a pre-hung door unit, installation is not too difficult. Put the unit in place and level it. It may be necessary to install shims around the frame to get it plumb. When the door is plumb, nail the jamb to the framed opening. Regardless of what you are installing, always read and follows the recommendations from the manufacturer of the product.

INSULATION

Insulation is not difficult to install, but it can irritate your skin. The easiest type to install for most remodeling jobs is batt insulation. This type of insulation is available in widths made to fit standard wall and joist cavities.

Wall insulation should have a vapor barrier. The barrier should be installed so that it is between the heated room and the insulation. You can buy rolls of batt insulation with a vapor

Figure 14.3   Plenty of light shines through the doors and windows of this kitchen. *Courtesy of Armstrong*

barrier already attached, or you can use unfaced insulation and install sheets of plastic as a vapor barrier. It is important to have the barrier facing the heated room, not the outside of the house. A strong stapler is the only tool needed for installing insulation.

> Never install the vapor barrier for insulation towards the outdoors. This can cause condensation and rotting of the insulation and wood members in a wall section.

DRYWALL

Other than dealing with the weight of the material, hanging drywall is not difficult. Finishing it, however, does take some time and practice. When installing new drywall in a kitchen, moisture-resistant products are a good idea. They are not normally required for kitchens, but they are a good idea. Let's take a look at what is involved with hanging and finishing drywall.

Drywall is available in different sizes. Professionals often use 4-x-12-foot sheets to reduce the number of seams in a job, but 4-x-8-foot sheets are much easier for the average person to handle. You can choose from different thicknesses to give your finished wall the proper depth.

Drywall can be hung with the use of nails or screws. Screws are less likely to work loose than nails. If screws are used, an electric screwdriver makes the job go much faster. Screws should be tight enough to make a depression in the wallboard. When nails are used, they should be driven extra deep to create a dimple in the drywall. The depressions will be filled with joint compound to hide the nail and screw heads.

Drywall can be cut with a drywall saw, jigsaw, or utility knife. Most pros use utility knives. The procedure requires the drywall to be scored with the utility knife and then broken at the scored seam. You can use a T-square, piece of lumber, or chalk line to make straight cuts.

Hanging drywall on a ceiling is physically the most difficult part of any drywall job. Ceilings should be hung before the walls are covered with drywall. When you drywall a ceiling, you will have to make cutouts for ceiling-mounted electrical boxes. Due to its weight, drywall is not easy to install above your head. However, there is a way to reduce this burden.

A T-brace will be of much assistance when hanging drywall on a ceiling. You can make a T-brace from scrap studs. To make the brace, nail a 2-x-4-foot piece of wood (about 3 feet long) onto the end of another 2 x 4 that is long enough to reach the ceiling, with a little left over.

The brace can be wedged under the drywall to hold it to the ceiling. The T-arm will rest under the drywall, and the long section of the brace will be wedged between the subfloor and the ceiling. It normally takes two people to raise drywall to the ceiling joists. Once the T-brace is wedged into place, it frees one of the people up to attach the drywall to the joists. Two braces can be used to free all hands for other work.

Hanging drywall on walls is much easier than on ceilings. The drywall can be hung vertically or horizontally. If you hang your walls vertically, you shouldn't need any help. Hanging the drywall horizontally generally results in fewer seams, but it is more difficult to do without a helper. There are, however, some tricks that make horizontal hanging easier for the sole remodeler.

Nail large nails to the studs to provide temporary support for the drywall panel. You can then rest the sheet of drywall on the nails while you attach it to the studs. The large nails can be removed once the drywall is secured.

A ledger can be used in place of nails for more uniform support of the drywall. Nail a 2 x 4 horizontally across the wall studs. Rest the drywall on the ledger while you attach it to the studs.

> It's possible to hang a ceiling by yourself. Sit the drywall on the tops of two ladders. Leave a couple of feet of the wallboard hanging over each end of the ladders. Put one T-brace under one end of the drywall and raise it with the brace. Wedge the brace against the floor and raise the other end of the drywall with another brace. This will take some time and practice, but once you get the hang of it, you can install your ceiling without help.

Outside corners of walls covered with drywall should be fitted with metal corner bead. The metal strips protect the exposed corners and edges. These strips are perforated and can be nailed or screwed to wall studs. The corner bead is designed to retain joint compound for a smooth finish.

Inside corners do not require metal corner bead. Drywall tape should be creased and installed to cover the seams of inside corners.

Taping the seams of new drywall is not difficult, but it may take a while to develop a feel for what you are doing. Buy joint compound that is premixed. The tape you will use to cover the

> When hanging drywall on the wall studs, don't forget to leave cutouts for electrical boxes, water supplies, drain arms, and other items that should not be covered up.

seams does not have an adhesive backing. It is held in place by the joint compound. A wide putty knife (about 4 inches wide) should be used to spread the joint compound over the tape, seams, and dimples.

The first coat of joint compound should be spread over seams, corner bead, and dimples. It is best to work one seam at a time. The first layer of compound should be about 3 inches wide, and it should be applied generously.

Once the compound covers a seam, lay a strip of tape on the compound and use a putty knife to work the tape down into the joint compound. The tape should sit deeply into the compound. Smooth out the compound and feather it away at the edges of the tape. Continue this process on all seams.

Tape is not necessary when filling nail dimples or covering corner bead. Simply apply joint compound in the depressions until it is flush with the drywall. Smooth the compound out with your putty knife and let it dry.

The first layer of joint compound should dry within 24 hours. A second layer will be applied on top of the first layer. It should be about twice as wide. The second layer must be left to dry for about 24 hours.

A third layer of compound is usually the final finish on drywall. Before applying the last coat of compound, you must sand the second layer you installed.

> New walls and ceilings should receive at least one coat of primer and one coat of paint. When buying your primer, ask the paint dealer to tint it to match the finish color.

Sand the compound first with medium-grit and then with fine-grit sandpaper. A good dust mask is very helpful during this job. A sanding block will make the job go faster and will be easier on your hands. Sand the compound with soft strokes to avoid scarring the walls.

When the second layer has been sanded properly, you may apply the third layer of compound. This last layer should be about 10 inches wide, and the edges should be feathered out. This final layer should be applied in a thin coat.

After the final layer has dried, it must be sanded. Use fine-grit sandpaper for the finish sanding. When this step is complete, you are ready to clean up and prepare to prime and paint the walls.

PAINT

Before you begin to paint, vacuum the room to remove all dust. If you don't, your paint will catch the dust, and the job will not look good. You will be working over a subfloor, so drop cloths are not necessary.

You must decide whether to use latex or oil paint. Latex cleans up better than oil, and it will do a fine job on your walls and ceiling. New walls and ceilings should receive at least one coat of primer and one coat of paint. When buying your primer, ask the paint dealer to tint it to match the finish color.

Most painters begin their work on the ceilings of a home. Paint rollers work well for applying paint and primer to ceilings. When you paint a ceiling with a roller, you have to cut in along the joints between the walls and ceiling with a brush. Use a 2- or 3-inch brush to apply a strip of paint to the edges of the ceiling. As soon as the strip of wet paint is applied, lay down the brush and pick up a roller. Use an extension handle on the roller to avoid numerous trips up and down a ladder.

> Roll paint on the ceiling and over the strip of fresh paint. Do the cut-in work a little at a time. Trying to cut in the whole ceiling before rolling on the paint will result in a mismatched finish. The cut-in strips will dry before the rest of the paint does. This results in two different finishes and looks strange. Roll paint on the ceiling in generous amounts, otherwise it will dry without covering the surface.

With the ceiling finished, you are ready to paint the walls. Apply cut-in strips of fresh paint around the tops of the walls. Follow the same procedures used on the ceiling to avoid mismatched paint.

After the first coat of paint or primer you may see imperfections that had been invisible. Take time between the first and second coat to touch up the drywall. Vacuum any dust created from the touch-up work before applying the second coat of paint.

You may wish to texture your ceiling. If so, there are many options available to you. Joint compound, just like that used to finish drywall, can be used to create a textured ceiling. Some types of paint are already texturized.

A variety of devices can be used to texture a ceiling. A stiff paintbrush can be used to create texture, and a stipple paint roller will also get the job done. Trowels can be used, and even common potato mashers are sometimes used to texture ceilings.

> Once your drywall is finished and ready for paint, prime it. One coat of primer will expose flaws in the finish work that you may not be able to see before the primer is applied.

The trim work around your windows, doors, and walls will also need to be painted or stained. Paint with a gloss finish is often used on trim when paint with a flat finish is used on walls. Kitchen walls are often painted with gloss paint. It is easier to clean than flat paint.

Before the final paint or stain can be applied to trim work, nail holes must be filled in with putty. Wood putty and a small putty knife are all that is needed for this job. If you will be staining the trim, use putty that will not show through the stain.

Trim is often stained or painted before it is installed. If you are going to stain your trim, be sure to get clear wood for the trim material. Trim can be stained with either a staining mitt or a brush. After the trim has been stained, you may wish to apply sealer over the stain. This is not a required step, but some people prefer the look and durability offered by sealants. Walls and ceilings are not particularly difficult to work with. However, they are important elements in a job and should be given the respect that they deserve.

15

Mechanical Work

Some types of mechanical modifications are generally required in all kitchen remodeling jobs. Not all renovations and alterations are big jobs, but even minor modifications can present major problems for inexperienced people.

A plumbing connection that is not made properly may blow apart, flooding the room being remodeled and the rest of the house. A mix-up in electrical wiring can be difficult to locate and can cause a number of problems. Moving a floor register to gain better heating can result in serious cuts from the sharp metal in ductwork.

Little jobs can create big problems. Most of the problems can be avoided and many of them are easy to correct, but you must have the right knowledge. Knowing this, let's look at what you may be involved with when working on your plumbing, heating, and electrical systems.

PLUMBING PIPES USED FOR DRAINS AND VENTS

There are many types of plumbing pipes that may be used for drains and vents. Most modern plumbing is done with plastic pipe, but older homes may be plumbed with pipes made from the following materials:

- Cast iron

- Galvanized steel

- Brass

- Lead

Some of these pipes do not perform well once they age. If you open up your walls during remodeling, it may pay to replace sections of your plumbing to avoid future problems. Let's look at the most common types of pipe found in remodeling jobs to see their strong points and weaknesses.

Cast-Iron Pipe

Cast-iron pipe can be found in houses of all ages. It has not been used in residential plumbing extensively since the mid-70s, but cast iron is still used today. If your home is more than thirty years old, there is a good chance it may have cast-iron drains and vents.

If you are forced to cut cast-iron pipe, you will be well served to rent a cutting tool for the job. It's possible to cut cast iron with a chisel or hacksaw, but a chain-type cutter is far easier and faster to work with. And, the cuts are cleaner.

Cast iron was typically used for large drains and vents. Galvanized-steel pipe was often used in conjunction with cast iron for small drains, such as those in kitchen sinks, bathtubs, and lavatories. You will most likely work with galvanized-steel pipe in simple remodeling jobs.

Cast-iron joints used to be made with oakum and molten lead, and they still are today. However, technology has delivered special rubber adapters for making connections with cast iron in modern installations. There are three basic types of rubber adapters. One type resembles a doughnut and is placed in the hub of one pipe so that the end of another pipe can be inserted, making a watertight joint. The other two types are used with cast-iron pipe that does not have hubs. These adapters slide over the ends of two pipes and are held in place with stainless-steel clamps. Not only is this type of connection much easier to make, it is also safer than working with hot lead.

Unless you are altering the main drainage and vent system in your home, it is unlikely that you will have to work with cast-iron pipe. But since you may wish to update the plumbing in your home, you may run into cast-iron pipe that you would like replaced. Let's take a quick look at how you can simplify the task of working with cast-iron pipe.

If you plan to cut cast-iron pipe, rent a ratchet-type soil-pipe cutter. This tool makes quick, easy work of cutting cast iron. All you have to do is wrap a special cutting chain around the pipe, secure the cutter, pump the handle a few times, and the pipe is cut cleanly. This is much easier than laboring your way through the pipe with a hacksaw.

> Cutting vertical sections of cast-iron pipe can be dangerous. If the pipe is not supported properly, the vertical piping could come crashing down on you. Before you cut a vertical pipe, make sure it is supported in a way to protect you.

Galvanized-Steel Pipe

If you have cast-iron pipe in you home, you probably also have some galvanized-steel pipe, too. This pipe tends to rust and build up blockages over the years. If you have the opportunity to replace

> If you want to convert a piece of cast-iron pipe to another type of pipe such as plastic pipe, use a universal rubber adapter for the conversion. This will make the job fast and simple.

galvanized pipe with plastic pipe, do it. You will be saving your-self from future trouble.

Galvanized pipe can be cut with a hacksaw, and the same rubber adapters used to join cast-iron and plastic pipe can be used on galvanized pipe.

DWV Copper

DWV copper was a popular drain and vent pipe for many years, and it is still found in many older homes. On the whole, copper drains and vents give very good service and should not need to be replaced. Copper drains and vents can be cut with a hacksaw, and the same universal adapters used with cast-iron and galvanized pipe can be used to convert copper to plastic.

Schedule-40 Plastic Pipe

Schedule-40 plastic pipe is the drain and vent pipe most often used in modern plumbing systems. There are two types of schedule-40 plastic pipe used in homes: ABS and PVC. ABS is black and PVC is white.

Both these pipes are easy to work with, and either can be cut with a hacksaw or a standard carpenter's saw. Joints for these pipes are normally made with a solvent or glue. Most plumbing codes recommend that a cleaner be used on plastic pipe and require that a primer be applied prior to gluing a joint. These pipes can be joined to any of the other types of drains and vents mentioned with universal rubber adapters.

PLUMBING PIPES FOR POTABLE WATER

Just as there are a number of approved drain and vent mate-rials, there are also several types of plumbing pipes for potable (drinking) water. Let's take a quick look at some of them.

Copper

Copper water pipe and tubing are found in more homes than any other type of water-distribution pipe. Copper is a dependable material that provides years of service. It can be cut with a hacksaw, but roller-cutters will cut the pipe much more smoothly. The joints for copper pipe and tubing are usually made by soldering. This can be a problem for some homeowners. Learning to solder watertight joints takes some time and experience. One way to avoid soldering is to use compression fittings.

Compression fittings are available in all shapes and sizes. They are easy to install, and they normally don't leak. If your joints are going to be concealed in a wall, compression fittings may not be a good idea, but they work well under sinks and in other accessible areas.

There is some risk that compression fittings will develop leaks as the pipes are vibrated with use. The leaks will be small and can be seen and corrected easily if they are visible. If, however, they are concealed in a wall, a small leak could go on for a long time, causing serious damage to building components before it is detected.

CPVC Pipe

CPVC pipe is another alternative for homeowners lacking soldering skills. CPVC is a rigid plastic pipe that is put together with solvent joints. A cleaner and primer should be used on the pipe and fittings prior to gluing joints.

When working with CPVC in cold temperatures, be careful not to drop the pipe on hard surfaces such as cement floors. CPVC tends to be very brittle under cold conditions. The pipe can crack if dropped. The crack may not be visible until the pipe is pressurized with water.

CPVC can be cut quite easily with a hacksaw, and it is simple to install. You should, however, allow plenty of time for joints to dry before moving the pipe. If a fresh joint is bumped or twisted before the glue has dried, a leak is likely.

PEX Pipe

Pex pipe is the new kid on the block. It is a flexible plastic pipe than can be installed much like electrical wiring. The pipe can be snaked through studs, and its flexibility allows for minimum joints.

If you opt for Pex pipe, you will need to rent a special crimping tool. Do not attempt to make joints with standard stainless-steel clamps. Pex joints require the use of insert fittings and special crimp rings. Many professional plumbers feel that Pex will eventually be more common than copper for potable water systems.

WHERE SHOULD YOU PUT YOUR PIPES?

Where should you put your pipes? The locations for pipes will vary with the type of fixtures being plumbed. Your plumbing supplier should be able to provide you with a rough-in book. The rough-in book will tell you exactly where to place your pipes. Exact rough-in measurements are usually not critical, but they can be, especially with fixtures such as pedestal lavatories. While it is impossible to predict exactly where your pipes should go without rough-in specifications, there are some rules-of-thumb that will normally work. Let's take a fixture-by-fixture look at where you might want to put your pipes.

Kitchen Sinks

The drains for kitchen sinks should come out of the wall about 15 inches above the subfloor. The drain should be near the center of the sink drain. If you are installing a double-bowl sink, you only need one drain line. A continuous waste will be used when the sink is installed that allows both bowls to empty into a single trap.

Water supplies for kitchen sinks should come out of the wall about 21 inches above the subfloor. The hot water should always be piped to the left side of the fixture. Most kitchen faucets are made with 8-inch centers. This means that your water pipes will be spaced 8 inches apart.

HEATING SYSTEM MODIFICATIONS

Heating system modifications are not needed in most kitchen remodeling jobs. Unless you are expanding the size of your room, the existing heat should be adequate and require no major work. However, there are times, especially with kitchen remodeling, when heat needs to be relocated within the room. Assuming that there is good access from under the kitchen floor, moving heat around is not normally a big job.

Ductwork is usually held together by metal strips that slide into a channel. These strips can be dislodged with a hammer. Metal-fabrication shops will be glad to make lengths of ductwork or offsets to your specifications. Other than the risk of cutting yourself on sharp metal, installing ductwork is not too difficult.

> Ductwork used in forced-hot-air heating and central air conditioning has very sharp edges when disassembled. If you are going to work with heating or air-conditioning ducts, wear gloves.

If you will be adding new ducts to an existing system or extending the length of existing ducts, talk with some professionals beforehand. Typically, the size of ductwork gets smaller as it goes along its route. If the duct is not sized properly, it cannot perform to its optimum output. These types of alterations may affect the effectiveness of your heating and cooling system. New ducts can be cut into existing trunk lines easily, but you must be sure your alterations will not strain your system.

> In some cases flexible ducts can be used to carry heat or cool air from a main trunk to an outlet register. Flexible duct is obviously easier to work with, and you are not as likely to hurt yourself.

Hot-water heat, in modern homes, runs through copper tubing similar if not identical to the type used for potable water distribution. Don't attempt to work with this type of heat unless you know how to solder. Before you cut into heating pipes, make sure the boiler is turned off and drained down to a point below the location on the pipes where you will be cutting.

There are two basic types of hot-water heating systems: one-pipe systems and two-pipe systems. In a one-pipe system, a supply pipe leaves the boiler and runs to the first heating unit. The water passes through the heating unit. When it comes out, it is conveyed to the next heating unit through more supply pipe. Some people refer to this as a loop system because the supply pipe makes a big loop through all the heating units and back to the boiler.

Two-pipe systems rely on supply pipes and return pipes. These systems are more costly due to the extra pipe involved, but they produce better heat. In these systems each heating unit receives a supply of hot water from one pipe, and another pipe immediately returns the water directly to the boiler.

Adding new heat to an expanded kitchen is certainly possible, but you must make sure the boiler is capable of heating the extra space. It would be very unlikely that any existing boiler couldn't handle the small amount of space being added for a kitchen, but you should make sure before altering the heating system.

After the new hot-water heating units are installed, you will need to bleed air out of the system. Professionals usually install special elbows, called vent ells or bleed ells, at individual heating units. These fittings are most commonly installed on the heat that has the highest elevation in the home. If your home has more than one story, bleed air from the highest heating units.

All you have to do in order to bleed air from the heating system is to cut the boiler on and remove the cap from a bleed fitting. You will probably hear air hissing out of the opening in the fitting. When the air is replaced with a stream of water, you have removed the air from the system.

It is customary with all types of heat to install it on exterior walls, usually under windows. If your house has an old heating system that works with steam or radiators, you should probably call in professionals to make the necessary changes in the system. These systems can be troublesome to work with, and it is not unusual for radiators and old steel pipes to fail and leak when disturbed.

ELECTRICAL SERVICES

Sometimes homeowners either want to or have to upgrade their electrical services for major remodeling projects. This is not normally the case with kitchen remodeling, but it can be. This is not a job you should do yourself unless you are a well-trained electrician with experience in working with panel boxes. All work with electricity poses some danger, but the risks involved with replacing a service panel are too great to take.

Installing New Electrical Boxes

Homeowners who are competent to work with electricity can install their own electrical boxes, but if you do not know what you are doing, leave all electrical work to licensed professionals. Poor workmanship with electrical wiring can result in fatal shocks and houses being burned to the ground. If you will be working with electrical boxes, here are some types and their uses:

- Switch boxes are usually rectangular. These boxes are commonly used for wall outlets and wall-mounted lights. The dimensions for rectangular boxes are generally 3 inches by 2 inches.
- Boxes used for ceiling lights are often octagonal. These boxes may also be used as junction boxes for joining numerous wires together. Each side of the boxes is

typically 4 inches long. Round boxes are also used for ceiling lights.

- Both octagonal and square boxes are used as junction boxes. Square boxes are more common and have typical dimensions of about 4 inches.

- Depth requirements for electrical boxes are determined by the number of wires to be placed in the box. Common depths vary from just over 1 inch to about 3½ inches.

If you are going to install your own electrical boxes, you must decide which types of boxes to use. The size and shape of electrical boxes vary with their purpose. Choose the proper type of box for the type of work that you will be doing with it.

Mounting Electrical Boxes

The mounting of electrical boxes can be done in a number of ways. Some boxes are sold with nails already inserted. All you have to do is position the box and drive the nail into a piece of wood. Other boxes have flanges that nails are driven through. Some boxes have flanges that move and allow more flexibility in terms of installation.

Boxes for ceiling fixtures are often nailed directly to ceiling joists. If the boxes need to be offset, such as in the middle of a joist bay, metal bars can be used to support the boxes. The metal bars are adjustable and mount between ceiling joists or studs. Once the bar is in place, the box can be mounted to the bar.

Rough-In Dimensions

Rough-in dimensions can be determined by local code requirements and the fixtures to be served. There are, however, some common rough-in figures you may be interested in knowing about.

Wall switches are usually mounted about 4 feet above the finished floor. Outlets are normally set between 12 and 18 inches above the floor and are spaced so that there is not more than 12 feet between outlets.

Where Does the Red Wire Go?

Where does the red wire go? What should be done with the black wire? These are questions many people have about wiring. Electrical wires are insulated with different colors for a purpose. The colors indicate what the wire is used for and where it should be attached.

Black and red wires are usually hot wires. White wires should be neutral, but they are sometimes used as hot wires. Don't trust any wire not to be hot. Green wires and plain copper wires are typically ground wires.

When matching colored wires to the screws in an electrical connection, they should be installed something like this. Black wires should connect to brass screws. Red wires should connect to brass or chrome screws. White wires are normally connected to chrome screws. Green wires and plain copper wires should connect to green screws.

Electrical wires should be crooked and placed under their respective screws in such a way that the crook in the wire will tighten with the screw. In other words, the end of the crooked wire should be facing in a clockwise position under the screw.

Wire nuts should be used when wires are twisted together. The colors of wire nuts indicate their size. Wire nuts are plastic on the outside and have wire springs on the inside. When wires are inserted into the wire nut, the nut can be turned clockwise to secure the wires. It is important to use a wire nut of the proper size, and it should be installed to a point where no exposed wiring is visible.

Ground Fault Interrupters

Ground fault interrupters (GFIs) are generally required in locations where a source of water is close to an electrical device. Kitchens are required to be equipped with GFI circuits or outlets. GFIs are safety devices. They kill the power to an electrical device if moisture is detected. It is possible to install GFI outlets or GFI circuit breakers. Check with your local code-enforcement office to determine the requirements in your area.

You should now have a fair understanding of what may be involved with mechanical modifications in your home. Never attempt to do any type of work that you are not sure you can do safely. The price of professionals is a much better option than doing harm to yourself or your house.

16

Cabinets, Countertops, Fixtures, Trim, and Appliances

Cabinets, countertops, fixtures, trim, and appliances must all be installed before your job will be finished. These aspects of the job play a vital role in how the finished job will look. They can also be more difficult to install than they appear to be. When you begin installing these items, you should be prepared to take your time. Carelessness in screw selection can cause you to puncture and ruin the surface of a new countertop or cabinet.

As you move toward the final phases of your job, you are likely to get excited by the thrill of completion. As you see all the cabinets installed in your kitchen, it can be tempting to work into the night to get the countertop installed. The desire to see the top installed before morning can be a mistake. If you are tired, you are more likely to make mistakes. The finish work in your project is very important. Don't rush it.

Of the items discussed in this chapter, cabinets are normally the first to be installed. Cabinet installation requires attention to detail, but it is a job most handy homeowners can handle. Let's begin our look at the finish phases of work with cabinets.

CHOOSING BASE CABINETS

Before you begin choosing base cabinets, you owe it to yourself to shop around. You may be amazed at the number of variations available. You will have decisions to make on sizes, styles, colors, and features.

Cabinets are fundamental elements of any working kitchen. They are likely to attract more attention than any other feature in the room. They will also receive a lot of use. Since you will want your kitchen to be beautiful, functional, and enjoyable to work in, take your time choosing the cabinets.

Standard base cabinets are generally about 32½ inches high. Once a countertop is installed on the base cabinets, the finished height is usually around 36 inches.

Base cabinets are available in different widths. The cabinet that will sit under the kitchen sink will normally be 5 feet wide. Other cabinets may be as narrow as 1 foot or as wide as 3 feet. There are, of course, other sizes available and custom cabinets can be made to your specifications.

Custom cabinets are generally much more expensive than production cabinets. With the wide selection of production cabinets available, there is rarely a need for custom cabinets. Some people want their cabinets built just for them, but most people will have no trouble finding stock cabinets to suit their needs and desires. It is your decision.

Cabinet materials can consist of solid wood, plywood, and particleboard. Many production cabinets use a mixture of these materials. Deciding on what you want your cabinets made of is only part of the buying decision. You will also have to look at the construction features of the cabinets. For example, dovetail joints should last longer than butt joints.

Other considerations for choosing base cabinets include whether the cabinet will have doors, drawers, appliance openings, or special accessories. An important consideration in choosing a drawer base is how well the drawers glide. Insist on a cabinet with quality glides and rollers.

> An important consideration in choosing a drawer base is how well the drawers glide. Insist on a cabinet with quality glides and rollers.

CHOOSING WALL CABINETS

Choosing wall cabinets will be similar to choosing base cabinets. You will have to consider the sizes and styles that best suit your requirements. What will you want your cabinets to offer? The questions you'll need to answer include the following:

Figure 16.1 Cabinet components. *Courtesy of Wellborn Cabinet, Inc.*

- Will your cabinets have glass doors?
- Do you want raised-panel doors?
- Will the cabinet doors have porcelain pulls?
- Do you prefer cabinet doors with finger grooves?
- There are plenty of choices to contemplate with cabinets.

Look for quality in the shelves and latches of wall cabinets. The supports for shelves should be adjustable and allow random spacing. Magnetic latches are usually favored over plastic latches. Inspect hinges, structural supports, and all other aspects of wall cabinets before you buy them.

The heights and widths of wall cabinets vary. Most wall cabinets are about 30 inches tall. The cabinets installed over refrigerators are frequently 15 inches tall, and wall cabinets installed over ranges are normally about 18 inches tall. Standard widths start around 12 inches and go up to 3 feet. Different manufacturers do offer cabinets in other sizes. When thinking of width, think in 3-inch increments, as this is how most wall cabinets are available.

30, 33, 36

Figure 16.2   Wall cabinets. *Courtesy of Wellborn Cabinet, Inc.*

CABINET INSTALLATION

Cabinet installation should begin with a design that you have studied and approved. It is much easier to make changes in a kitchen design on a drafting table or computer than it is in the kitchen. You should have a good cabinet layout already drawn. Any good cabinet supplier will provide recommended designs and drawings. When you are ready to install your cabinets, follow the design. But before you jump right into setting and hanging cabinets, double-check your previous work.

Check your floor and walls to make sure they are plumb and level. Cabinets that are not installed level may not operate properly, and there may be visual evidence of the poor installation. Shims can be used to overcome minor problems with walls and floors, but you should know what you are dealing with before you begin installing your cabinets.

Wall Cabinets

Install wall cabinets first. By installing the wall cabinets first, you reduce the risk of damaging base cabinets and you will have more freedom of movement for the job.

There are no rules to indicate how high you must hang your wall cabinets, but most are hung so that the tops are about 84 inches above the floor. Once you determine the desired height for your cabinets, mark a level line as a reference point.

Before you put the cabinets in place, find the wall studs. If you have gutted your kitchen and installed new drywall, you will be familiar with the stud locations. You may have even thought ahead and marked their location on your kitchen plan for easy reference.

Begin the installation process by hanging a corner cabinet. Cabinet installation is much easier when at least two people

If you have trouble locating the studs, don't hesitate to probe the wall where the cabinets will be hung. The back of the cabinet will conceal any holes you make in the wall.

are working on the job. Many professionals place props under the cabinets they are hanging to help keep the units in place prior to permanent attachment. The props can be made from lumber you have left over from the rough carpentry work.

When the first cabinet is in place and level, drill holes through the back of the cabinet and into the wall studs. The holes should be kept near the top of the cabinet. Most cabinets have mounting strips for the screws to penetrate. Install screws to hold the cabinet in place. Check the unit to make sure it is level and plumb. If it isn't, use shims to install the cabinet properly.

With the first cabinet installed, you are ready to install adjacent cabinets in the same manner. Adjacent cabinets should be attached to each other. Make sure the cabinets are aligned uniformly. Use small screws to attach the two cabinets to each other. The screws should be installed near the top and bottom of the cabinet sidewalls.

If you have help available, you may want to put the cabinets together on the floor and then raise them to the wall as one unit. Take your time in aligning the cabinets. When the cabinets are attached, simply raise them to the wall and support them with prop sticks. Position the cabinets so that they are level and plumb, and then screw them to the wall studs. If you have chosen to install a valance, do it before you set the base cabinets.

> Not all base cabinets have sides and backs. Some are just fronts. This type of unit requires the installation of cleats. Cleats are just strips of wood that support the countertop. The cleats should be attached to wall studs with the top of the cleat at the same height as the tops of adjacent cabinets.

Base Cabinets

When installing base cabinets, start with a corner cabinet and build out with the remaining cabinets. Base cabinets should be attached to each other in the same way as wall cabinets. Check frequently to see that the base cabinets are level and plumb. It may be necessary to shim under the cabinets to keep them level.

Figure 16.3   Base cabinets. *Courtesy of Wellborn Cabinet, Inc.*

COUNTERTOP INSTALLATION

Once you have your base cabinets set, you will want to install the countertop. Some people wait until the base cabinets are installed to order their countertops. Working in this manner slows down the progression of the job, but it eliminates much of the risk of getting a countertop that is not sized properly. If you are buying your cabinets and countertop from a good supplier, your kitchen layout was probably drawn well in advance, and it is likely you already have the countertop. Assuming that you have your counter, let's see how it should be installed.

Look down on your base cabinets. You should see some triangular blocks of wood in the corners. These triangles provide a place to attach the counter to the cabinet. Before setting the counter in place, drill holes through these mounting blocks. Keep the holes in a location that will allow you to install screws from inside the cabinet. You may want to drill the

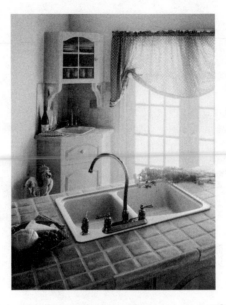

Figure 16.4   Ceramic tile countertop. *Photo courtesy of Moen, Inc.*

Figure 16.5   Granite countertop with double bowl sink. *Photo courtesy of Moen, Inc.*

Figure 16.6 Countertop with double bowl sink. *Photo courtesy of Moen, Inc.*

holes on an angle towards the center of the cabinet. This will make the installation of screws easier.

Position the countertop on the base cabinets and check its fit. When you are satisfied with the positioning of the top, install screws from below. The screws used should be long enough to penetrate the triangular blocks and the bottom of the countertop, but be certain they are not long enough to come through the surface of the counter and ruin it.

Kitchen counters must have a hole cut for the kitchen sink. The supplier of the top will often cut this hole if he or she is provided with information on the size of the sink. If you must cut your own sinkhole, use the template that came with your new sink. If you don't have a template to work with, turn the sink upside down and set it in place on the counter.

Lightly trace around the sink rim with a pencil. Remove the sink and draw a new outline inside the original tracing. The hole must be smaller than the lines you traced around the sink.

There must be enough counter left after the hole is cut to support the rim of the sink.

When you are ready to cut out the sinkhole, drill a hole in the countertop within the perimeter of the sinkhole. Use a jigsaw to cut out the hole. Put the blade in the hole you drilled and slowly cut the hole. Remember, the hole you make must be smaller than the outline of the sink. After the hole is cut, set the sink in it and check the fit. You may have to enlarge the hole a little at a time to get a perfect fit.

INSTALLATION OF INTERIOR TRIM

The installation of interior trim is not difficult, but it does require precise measurements and patience. A miter box and back saw will be needed for cutting the angles required for interior trim. A compound miter saw is a better option. You can buy such saws for a few hundred dollars. Your decision depends upon whether you are willing to use elbow grease with a back saw or if you prefer an electrical saw. Once you get the hang of cutting angles, installing trim won't be much of a chore.

Baseboard trim should be nailed to wall studs with small finish nails. When baseboard trim meets a door casing or a cabinet, it simply butts against it. Shoe molding is generally installed with baseboard trim when vinyl flooring is used. Shoe molding is small trim that is installed in front of baseboard trim. It is often used to cover the joints where vinyl flooring meets a baseboard. If the flooring was installed before the baseboard trim, shoe molding is not necessary.

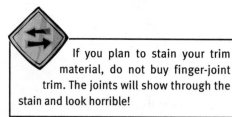

If you plan to stain your trim material, do not buy finger-joint trim. The joints will show through the stain and look horrible!

Windows, doors, and open entryways are often trimmed with casing. The only trick to installing this trim is in cutting the proper angles, and a miter box or miter saw will make that part of the job nearly foolproof.

The nails installed in trim should be countersunk. A nail punch can be used to drive the nail heads deep into the trim. Putty should then be placed in the nail holes before the final paint or stain work is done. If the trim is to be stained, make sure it is made of clear wood and that the putty will not show through the stain.

SETTING PLUMBING FIXTURES

When you are ready for setting plumbing fixtures, the end of your job is in sight. Some plumbing fixtures must be handled with care, but the installation of most plumbing fixtures is not very difficult. Let's see what is involved with the installation of common kitchen plumbing fixtures.

INSTALLING KITCHEN SINKS

Some kitchen sinks are drop-ins. Drop-in sinks don't require clips—only caulking. Most sinks, however, are held in place with clips. These clips slide into a channel that runs around the rim of the sink. As the clips are tightened, usually with a screwdriver, the clips bite into the bottom of the countertop pulling the sink firmly into contact with the top of the counter. There are different types of sink clamps, so check your materials and manufacturer's instructions for proper installation.

Kitchen sinks utilize basket strainers for drains. Putty is applied around the rim of the drain, and the drain is pushed through the hole in the sink. From below, a gasket is slid over the threaded portion of the drain, and a large nut is applied and tightened. These nuts can be difficult to tighten without help. It is best to have someone cross screwdrivers in the crossbars of the basket strainer as the nut is being tightened. Otherwise the entire drain assembly tends to turn without becoming tight.

A good solution for the person working alone is a type of drain that uses a flange to secure the basket strainer. With this type of arrangement, the flange slides over the threads and is held against the bottom of the sink by three pressure points. The pressure points are threaded rods, extending from another flange that is screwed onto the drain threads. As the threaded rods are tightened, they apply pressure and seal the drain.

Kitchen tailpieces do not screw into the basket strainers. Instead, they are flanged to accept tailpiece washers. The nylon washer sits on top of the tailpiece, and the tailpiece is held in place with a slip-nut.

Since many kitchen sinks have two bowls, continuous wastes are often used to drain the two bowls to a common trap. There are end-outlet and center-outlet wastes. The continuous waste attaches to the sink's tailpieces with slip-nuts and washers. Then the waste tubes run either to a tee for an end-outlet waste or a double tee for a center outlet waste. The bottoms of these tees accept a tailpiece and allow the trap to be attached.

APPLIANCES

Appliances are a natural part of any kitchen. Ranges and refrigerators are easy to install. If you follow the manufacturer's recommendations for these items, you should be able to install them with ease. However, dishwashers and garbage disposers are combined with both plumbing and electrical systems, and it may help to have a little extra information on these appliances.

Garbage Disposers

Garbage disposers are mounted to kitchen sinks and take the place of a basket strainer. Putty is applied to the ring of the disposer's trim piece before the trim is pushed through the drain hole. A pressure-type flange is put over the collar of the drain and followed by a snap ring. The snap ring holds the pressure flange in place. Threaded rods are tightened with a screwdriver

Figure 16.7   Typical garbage disposer installation with hot water dispenser. *Courtesy of In-Sink-Erator*

Figure 16.8   Garbage disposer unit. *Courtesy of In-Sink-Erator*

to seal the drain. The disposer is held in place and a rotating collar is turned to lock the disposer firmly to the sink flange.

Disposers come with small ells. Two screws are loosened on the side of the disposer. The ell fits through a metal housing and a rubber washer is placed on the beveled end of the ell, the short end. The metal housing is put back in place and the screws are tightened. This compresses the gasket between the face of the ell and the side of the disposer. Then a continuous waste or trap is connected to the bottom of the disposer ell.

Dishwashers

Dishwashers are normally installed under countertops between cabinets. There are metal tabs at the top of dishwashers that allow screws to be installed to hold the appliance in place. A rubber drain hose connects to a ridged nylon drain on the appliance. The hose is held in place by a snap ring or clamp. This hose should run into the sink base and rise to the top of the enclosure. It should connect to an air gap with clamps.

If you are connecting to a disposer, you must knock out the factory-installed plug before connecting the hose. This can be done with a sturdy screwdriver and a hammer. You should knock this plug out before installing the disposer. Otherwise, retrieving the knocked-out plug will be difficult.

An air gap is a device that sits on the counter and has a chrome cover. It is installed by removing the chrome cover and mounting nut. The unit is pushed up through a hole from beneath the counter. Then a gasket and mounting nut are installed and tightened. Afterwards the chrome cover is replaced. Below the counter the air gap splits off into a wye.

The small hose from the dishwasher connects to one side of the wye and is held in place with a clamp. A larger hose is run from the other section of the wye to a wye-tailpiece connection or a connection point on a disposer. If you are connecting to a disposer, you must knock out the factory-installed plug before connecting the hose. This can be done with a sturdy screwdriver and a hammer. You should knock this plug out before installing the disposer. Otherwise, retrieving the knocked-out plug will be difficult.

To connect the water supply to the dishwasher, you need to use a dishwasher stop or cut a tee into the hot-water supply to the sink. A dishwasher stop has provisions for a supply tube to the sink and the tubing running to the dishwasher. The copper tubing for the dishwasher should be equipped with a cut-off valve. If you use a dishwasher stop, you have a built-in cut-off. If you cut in a tee, install a cut-off valve between the tee and the dishwasher.

The tubing will run to a point under the dishwasher. A dishwasher ell is used to make the connection between the tubing and the dishwasher. The dishwasher ell screws into the dishwasher. Use pipe dope or tape on the threads. The tubing connects to the ell with a compression nut and ferrule.

INSTALLING ELECTRICAL FIXTURES AND DEVICES

Installing electrical fixtures and devices is quite simple, but caution must be observed due to the risk of electrocution. Never trust a wire until it has been tested with a meter.

Installing Wiring Devices

When installing wiring devices, there is a color-code system that should be followed. Green wires or bare copper wires should be used as ground wires and attached to green screws. Red wires should be considered hot wires and will normally attach to brass or chrome screws. Black wires are also considered hot and generally attach to brass screws. In many cases white wires serve as a neutral wire and connect to chrome screws, but they can be hot.

Wall Plates and Switch Covers

Wall plates and switch covers simply mount over outlet boxes and switch boxes. They are held in place with screws.

Installing Light Fixtures

Installing light fixtures is usually a matter of matching up feed wires with fixture wires and mounting the fixture. Most fixtures have threaded studs that hold them to their electrical box. Consult the directions that come with your light fixtures and follow the manufacturer's recommendations.

This has been a long chapter, but you should have learned a great deal. With all this work out of the way, you may feel like you are home free, but don't relax too much. The last few days of a job are when many accidents happen. Stay alert, stay safe, and be happy.

Index

Page numbers in italics refer to figures and tables